A Miscellany  OF Murder

A Miscellany of Murder

From History and Literature to
True Crime and Television,
A KILLER SELECTION OF TRIVIA

Executed by
The Monday Murder Club

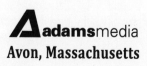

adamsmedia
Avon, Massachusetts

Published by
Adams Media, a division of F+W Media, Inc.
57 Littlefield Street, Avon, MA 02322. U.S.A.
www.adamsmedia.com

ISBN 10: 1-4405-2593-5
ISBN 13: 978-1-4405-2593-3
eISBN 10: 1-4405-3019-X
eISBN 13: 978-1-4405-3019-7

Printed in the United States of America.

10 9 8 7 6 5 4 3 2 1

Library of Congress Cataloging-in-Publication Data
is available from the publisher.

This publication is designed to provide accurate and authoritative information with regard to the subject matter covered. It is sold with the understanding that the publisher is not engaged in rendering legal, accounting, or other professional advice. If legal advice or other expert assistance is required, the services of a competent professional person should be sought.

—From a *Declaration of Principles* jointly adopted by a Committee of the American Bar Association and a Committee of Publishers and Associations

Many of the designations used by manufacturers and sellers to distinguish their product are claimed as trademarks. Where those designations appear in this book and Adams Media was aware of a trademark claim, the designations have been printed with initial capital letters.

This book is available at quantity discounts for bulk purchases.
For information, please call 1-800-289-0963.

To mystery lovers and true crime aficionados everywhere

FOREWORD

The Monday Murder Club had me in mind when they assembled this mind-boggling collection of murder-inspired miscellany from life and literature, television and film. My fascination with murder goes back, way back, long before I started to write crime fiction.

In 1958, America was riveted by news that glamorous movie star Lana Turner's daughter Cheryl Crane had murdered her mother's handsome boyfriend, small-time hood Johnny Stompanato. I'd just turned ten years old and was oblivious to most current events. But that news story got my attention. After all, Cheryl Crane was just four years older than me and the drama took place in a second-floor bedroom in a house two blocks from where we lived in Beverly Hills.

I still remember the stark, black-and-white photographs of Stompanato's corpse lying on plush carpeting. I feasted on the ghoulish details: the eight-inch carving knife; the severed aorta; the pink bedroom; the too-big wool coat (covering bloodstained clothing, I always assumed); and the white head scarf that Cheryl wore when the police led her away. These bits of trivia are still stuck in my mind so many years later.

The coroner's inquest was broadcast live on television. How could we all not marvel at how life was imitating fiction? After all, Lana Turner was at the same time appearing in the movie *Peyton Place* in which she played a single mother. One of her big scenes was a courtroom interrogation. Meanwhile, in real life, Lana Turner testified as the only witness, giving what reporters called the performance of a lifetime. Her daughter got off with a verdict of "justifiable homicide."

I imagined what it must have been like that night for young Cheryl, growing more and more frightened as Stompanato beat and threatened her mother. I could visualize myself in her place, going into the kitchen, pulling open a drawer and selecting the longest knife. She must have rehearsed what she was going to do as she crept back up the stairs. Then she must have stood in the upstairs hallway, screwing up her courage.

That's when the mystery writer I didn't even know I had in me kicked in, and I wondered: What if Cheryl didn't kill Johnny Stompanato? What if she confessed to protect her mother? If the murder ever gets made into a biopic, and heaven only knows why it hasn't, I won't be surprised if the same question gets raised.

At the same time that I was imagining myself as Cheryl Crane, I was playing marathon rounds of Clue (Mr. Green with the dagger in the lounge) and devouring Nancy Drew books. My copies were the blue hardback edition that portrayed Nancy as rich, headstrong, and reckless, before later editions sanded the eighteen-year-old girl detective's edges. My favorite was #2, *The Hidden Staircase*. In it, Nancy breaks into a house, then trips and falls through a loose panel into a secret staircase which she follows to an underground tunnel connecting two mansions.

I loved Nancy Drew stories because they were scary and safe at the same time. Their massive coincidences and implausibilities never bothered me a bit, nor did the fact that the plots often involved murder. Reading one of those novels was like getting on a scary carnival ride that you know will deliver you, in the end, to a safe place.

I went on to read all of Sherlock Holmes. Then I churned through the complete works of Agatha Christie, Dorothy L. Sayers, Ngaio Marsh, and P. D. James. I was addicted to the Perry Mason television series, each week trying to guess who the killer was before the reveal in the next-to-final scene in the courtroom, after which Perry and Paul Drake (both smoking) and Della Street (not) went back to the office and recapped the clues.

I've been devouring murder mysteries—real and fictional—ever since. Fortunately, and for this I thank my lucky stars, I've never experienced murder firsthand. *Miscellany of Murder* is the perfect tonic for this murder maven's peaceful and blessedly quotidian life.

Hallie Ephron is the author of the suspense novels *Come and Find Me* (2011) and *Never Tell a Lie* (2009), which was made into the movie *And Baby Will Fall* (2011) for the Lifetime Movie Network. She also reviews murder mysteries for *The Boston Globe* and wrote *Writing and Selling Your Mystery Novel: How to Knock 'Em Dead with Style* (2005).

CONTENTS

ACKNOWLEDGMENTS

We'd like to thank each other, first and foremost. It was criminally fun to work on this project together—and we did so on a very tight timeline without coming to blows.

We'd like to acknowledge our families for indulging us in what many might consider an unseemly obsession with murder. And of course we'd like to thank all the great folks at Adams Media, especially Victoria Sandbrook, Matthew Glazer, Meredith O'Hayre, Casey Ebert, Sylvia McArdle, Elisabeth Lariviere, Karen Cooper, and last, but most certainly not least, Gina Panettieri and all the folks at the Talcott Notch Literary Services.

INTRODUCTION

Murder

n., from the Old English *morthor*, meaning death

1. The premeditated, unlawful killing of one person by another person
2. A cruel killing
3. Devastation; ruin
4. Misery; agony
5. A flock of crows

"Murder is unique in that it abolishes the party it injures, so that society has to take the place of the victim and on his behalf demand atonement or grant forgiveness; it is the one crime in which society has a direct interest." —**W. H. AUDEN**

To say that as a society we take an interest in murder is an understatement. From today's headlines to tomorrow's books, TV, and movies, murder reigns supreme. And as if the more than half a million real-life murders a year around the globe (some 17,000 in 2010 in the United States alone) some-how constituted a lack of violent death, we make up for that lack in fiction—adding a never-ending supply of made-up stories of murder and mayhem to the count.

To paraphrase P. D. James, our fascination with this worst of crimes—a crime against the very humanity of our fellow humanity—perhaps lies more with our desire to restore order than it does with the despicable act itself. At any rate, fascinated we are—and remain.

A Miscellany of Murder is designed to satisfy that desire—one corpse at a time. Enjoy—and we mean that in a good, thoroughly lawful way.

The Monday Murder Club

"*The Bible and several other self-help or enlightenment books cite the Seven Deadly Sins. They are: pride, greed, lust, envy, wrath, sloth, and gluttony. That pretty much covers everything that we do, that is sinful . . . or fun for that matter.*" —DAVE MUSTAINE

LUST

n., from the Old High German *lust,* meaning pleasure

1. Severe or uncontrollable sexual craving
2. An overwhelming desire
3. Extreme eagerness or enthusiasm

"Lust is to the other passions what the nervous fluid is to life; it supports them all, lends strength to them all; ambition, cruelty, avarice, revenge, are all founded on lust." —**MARQUIS DE SADE**

Lust for sex. Lust for power. Lust for life—and death. The Marquis de Sade knew whereof he spoke. As the first of the seven deadly sins, lust commands a special place in the lexicon of transgression. It's a trigger-happy emotion that can turn from inarticulate ardor to homicidal mania on a dime. Lust is the sin that drives ordinary people to extraordinary measures, one corpse—or more—at a time.

KILLER WIT

"Give them pleasure—the same pleasure they have when they wake up from a nightmare."

—ALFRED HITCHCOCK

Arresting Men in Uniform

Match the sexy TV cop with the actor who brings him to life on the screen:

1. Pete Cochran (*The Mod Squad*, 1968–1973)
2. Linc Hayes (*The Mod Squad*, 1968–1973)
3. Assistant Inspector Steve Keller (*The Streets of San Francisco*, 1972–1977)
4. Detective David Michael Starsky (*Starsky and Hutch*, 1975–1979)
5. Detective Kenneth "Hutch" Hutchinson (*Starsky and Hutch*, 1975–1979)
6. Officer Francis (Frank) "Ponch" Poncherello (*CHiPs*, 1977–1983)
7. Detective Sonny Crockett (*Miami Vice*, 1984–1990)
8. Detective Ricardo Tubbs (*Miami Vice*, 1984–1990)
9. Officer Tom Hanson (*21 Jump Street*, 1987–1990)
10. Detective John Kelly (*NYPD Blue*, 1993–1994)
11. Detective Bobby Simone (*NYPD Blue*, 1994–1998, 2004)
12. Detective Jimmy McNulty (*The Wire*, 2002–2008)

a. Philip Michael Thomas
b. David Soul
c. Dominic West
d. Michael Cole
e. Don Johnson
f. David Caruso
g. Michael Douglas
h. Erik Estrada
i. Jimmy Smits
j. Paul Michael Glaser
k. Johnny Depp
l. Clarence Williams III

ANSWERS: 1-d; 2-l; 3-g; 4-j; 5-b; 6-h; 7-e; 8-a; 9-k; 10-f; 11-i; 12-c

Since When Doesn't Hollywood Like Blonds?

Dashiell Hammett described Sam Spade as the "blond Satan."

- In *The Maltese Falcon* (1931), Sam Spade was played by Ricardo Cortez.
- In *Satan Met a Lady* (1936), a thinly disguised rehash of *The Maltese Falcon*, Warren William filled the role under the character name "Ted Shane."
- Finally, Humphrey Bogart defined Sam Spade in the 1941 version of *The Maltese Falcon*.

None of the men were blond.

"If you live in rock and roll, as I do, you see the reality of sex, of male lust and women being aroused by male lust. It attracts women. It doesn't repel them." —CAMILLE PAGLIA

Lust for Death

Jane Toppan liked to climb into bed with her dying patients and hold them close as they began to slip away from the world of the living. In fact, she liked to overdose them with morphine, then bring them back from the brink of death with atropine before finally killing them off for good.

Toppan, born in Boston in 1857, worked as a nurse at Cambridge Hospital and Massachusetts General Hospital before embarking on a twenty-year career as a private nurse and murderer. She finally overreached herself in 1901, when four members of one family died under her care in a six-week period. All were given lethal amounts of morphine. When apprehended, Toppan confessed to killing thirty-one people and said she was sexually aroused by the act of killing-reviving-killing. She was confined to a state mental institution until she died at age eighty-one.

Belladonna

n.: In Italian a beautiful lady; in English a deadly poison. A striking example of the essential identity of the two tongues. —AMBROSE BIERCE, *DEVIL'S DICTIONARY* (1911)

The Quotable P.I. _____

Adrienne Fromsett: *Do you fall in love with all of your clients?*
Philip Marlowe: *Only the ones in skirts.*
—ROBERT MONTGOMERY AS PHILIP MARLOWE AND AUDREY TOTTER AS ADRIENNE FROMSETT IN *LADY IN THE LAKE* (1947)

"For those for whom the sex act has come to seem mechanical and merely the meeting and manipulation of body parts, there often remains a hunger which can be called metaphysical but which is not recognized as such, and which seeks satisfaction in physical danger, or sometimes in torture, suicide, or murder." —MARSHALL MCLUHAN

Not Guilty by Reason of Blondness

If you're a woman convicted of a crime, go blond. Blond defendants are less likely to be convicted of a crime—especially if they're of the blue-eyed, full-lipped variety. The only exception: crimes of unintentional negligence, in which case a blond is more likely to be found guilty. Go figure. (Source: ICM)

"The body is meant to be seen, not all covered up." —MARILYN MONROE

A Woman's Touch: A Few Female Detectives from Film Noir

- Florence Dempsey, *Mystery of the Wax Museum* (1933)
- Torchy Blane, *Smart Blonde* (1937)
- Carol "Kansas" Richman, *Phantom Lady* (1944)
- Catherine Bennett, *Black Angel* (1946)
- Eleanor Johnson, *Woman on the Run* (1950)
- Cary Scott, *All That Heaven Allows* (1955)

> *"You're wrong, boys. Hold-ups and murder are my meat. Here's the open sesame that swings wide all portals—my press pass. Torchy Blane of the Star."* —LOLA LANE AS TORCHY BLANE IN *PANAMA* (1938)

The Birth of a Character, the Death of Her Creator

In *The Girl with the Dragon Tattoo* (2008), Swedish unknown Stieg Larsson created one of the most affecting, antisocial, archetypal heroines of all time—and then he died suddenly of a heart attack before his Lisbeth novels were published. Those who know Lisbeth Salander are not surprised that her creator should have paid such a high price for bringing his private computer-hacking, revenge-seeking, smoking-hot tattooed wet dream to life. There are those who claim that his death was not due to natural causes. It is safe to say that only Lisbeth Salander knows for sure. In her world, living on your own terms always costs you everything but your soul.

Is That a Nightstick or Are You Just Happy to See Me?

In the following movies, law enforcement officers make bad relationship choices. Can you name them?

1. Richard Dreyfuss plays Seattle Detective Chris Lecce who falls for Maria McGuire (Madeleine Stowe), the girlfriend of a wanted fugitive.
2. Debra Winger plays undercover FBI agent Catherine Weaver who falls for suspect Gary Simmons (Tom Berenger).
3. Al Pacino plays NYPD Detective Frank Keller who falls for suspect Helen Cruger (Ellen Barkin).
4. Keanu Reeves plays undercover FBI agent Johnny Utah who falls for the surfer life-style of Bodhi (Patrick Swayze), who may be a bank robber.
5. Michael Douglas plays Detective Nick Curran who falls for suspect Catherine Tramell (Sharon Stone).

5. *Basic Instinct* (1992)

ANSWERS: 1. *Stakeout* (1987); 2. *Betrayed* (1988); 3. *Sea of Love* (1989); 4. *Point Break* (1991);

The Quotable P.I.

Mike Church: *I'm not looking for Ms. Right, I'm looking for Ms. Right Now.*

—KENNETH BRANAGH AS P.I. MIKE CHURCH IN *DEAD AGAIN* (1991)

✑ First Lines

"Nancy Frail had been a whore of a sort.

"Whoredom is a business. It has a high level of profitability, the overhead being minimal. Its practice needs only a man with a lust and the money to gratify it. And the right kind of woman. Some of them are craftswomen at their trade; others have all the response and skill of a badly stuffed pillow." —*HERE LIES NANCY FRAIL* (1972) BY JONATHAN ROSS

Where Would Prostitution Be Without the Johns?

Match the P.I.s named John with their creators:

1. John Bodie
2. John Caine
3. John Cuddy
4. John Dalmas
5. John Denson
6. John Locke
7. John Rankin
8. John Shaft
9. John J. Shannon
10. John Marshall Tanner

a. James Grady
b. Richard Hoyt
c. John L. Ketchum
d. Cleve F. Adams
e. Jeremiah Healy
f. Mike Pettit
g. Stephen Greenleaf
h. Charles Knief
i. Ernest Tidyman
j. Raymond Chandler

ANSWERS: 1-c; 2-h; 3-e; 4-j; 5-b; 6-f; 7-a; 8-i; 9-d; 10-g

> *"They have turned on each other with a vengeance, these two once-fervid lovers. There is no doubt they hate each other thoroughly."*
> —DAMON RUNYON, "THE ETERNAL BLONDE" (1927)

Death Is Like a Box of Chocolates

Mary Dunning and her guests didn't know what they were going to get when they dug into the box of chocolates delivered to her family's Delaware home with the note, "With love to yourself and baby.—Mrs. C." The four ladies and two children who shared the candy that August evening in 1898 all became violently ill, and within days Mrs. Dunning and one of her guests were dead from arsenic poisoning.

The note and chocolates were easily traced to Cordelia Botkin of San Francisco, longtime lover of Mary's husband, John, even when the family was living together in California. Dunning had recently broken off with Mrs. Botkin and taken a job as a war correspondent in Puerto Rico. She did not take it well.

Cordelia Botkin was tried in San Francisco and sentenced to life in prison. While in jail pending an appeal of her sentence, she was found to be "on intimate terms" with two guards who furnished her with luxuries and even escorted her on outings. She was not as happy in San Quentin and died in 1910 from "softening of the brain due to melancholy."

> *"It's only in love and in murder that we still remain sincere."*
> —FRIEDRICH DÜRRENMATT, *INCIDENT AT TWILIGHT* (1952)

P.Eye Candy for Her
- Efrem Zimbalist Jr. as Stuart "Stu" Bailey and Roger Smith as Jeff Spencer (*77 Sunset Strip*, 1958–1964)
- James Garner as Jim Rockford (*The Rockford Files*, 1974–1980)
- Tom Selleck as Thomas Magnum (*Magnum P.I.*, 1980–1988)
- Pierce Brosnan as Remington Steele (*Remington Steele*, 1982–1987)
- Robert Urich as Spenser (*Spenser: For Hire*, 1985–1988)

> *"Murder offers the promise of vast relief. It is never unsexual."*
> —NORMAN MAILER, *AN AMERICAN DREAM* (1965)

COP TALK: SEX, LIES, AND VIDEOTAPE

(Riggs and Rika are in bed.)

Martin Riggs: *I think it's time for the seventh inning stretch.*

Riggs: *That's a baseball expression.*

Rika van den Haas: *I know. But we're only up to the fourth inning.*

Riggs: *Batter up!*

—MEL GIBSON AS SERGEANT MARTIN RIGGS AND PATSY KENSIT AS RIKA VAN DEN HAAS IN *LETHAL WEAPON 2* (1989)

Arresting Women in Uniform

Match the sexy TV cop with the actress who brings her to life on the screen:

1. Julie Barnes (*The Mod Squad*, 1968–1973)

2. Sergeant Suzanne "Pepper" Anderson (*Police Woman*, 1974–1978)

3. Stacy Sheridan (*T.J. Hooker*, 1982–1986)

4. DCI Jane Tennison (*Prime Suspect*, 1991–1996, 2003–2006)

5. Detective Olivia Benson (*Law & Order: Special Victims Unit*, 1999–)

6. Catherine Willows (*CSI: Crime Scene Investigation*, 2000–)

7. Special Agent Samantha Spade (*Without a Trace*, 2002–2009)

8. Detective Lilly Rush (*Cold Case*, 2003–2010)

9. Probation Officer Tina Hanlon (*The Shield*, 2006–2008)

10. Detective Dani Reese (*Life*, 2007–2009)

11. Detective Kate Beckett (*Castle*, 2009–)

a. Sarah Shahi

b. Mariska Hargitay

c. Paula Garcés

d. Poppy Montgomery

e. Angie Dickinson

f. Kathryn Morris

g. Peggy Lipton

h. Stana Katic

i. Helen Mirren

j. Heather Locklear

k. Marg Helgenberger

ANSWERS: 1-g; 2-e; 3-j; 4-i; 5-b; 6-k; 7-d; 8-f; 9-c; 10-a; 11-h

✑ *First Lines*

"I think I am the long-haired, long-legged blonde though, torn between excitement and alarm, about to have my first affair with a married man."
—*MEN IN BLUE* (BADGE OF HONOR SERIES #1, 1988) BY W. E. B. GRIFFIN

The Trouble with Blondes

According to a 2010 study by the University of California, blonde women are more aggressive than redheads or brunettes, thanks to a confidence borne of their yellow locks. That said, blondes are the least likely to actually get into a fight—presumably a result of the reluctance to muss their fair hair.

Which may explain why the troublemakers in mysteries—from Raymond Chandler novels to Alfred Hitchcock movies—are usually the golden girls.

> *"Any woman can fool a man if she wants to and if he's in love with her."*
> —AGATHA CHRISTIE

The Live-In Lover

'Tis a thin line between tragedy and farce.

Take the case of the mismatched lovers, Walburga "Vally" Osterreich and Otto Sanhuber, accused in 1922 of killing Vally's husband, Fred. Vally was a lusty, statuesque woman married to a corpulent apron manufacturer. Otto was a short, skinny sewing machine repairman young enough to be her son. For fourteen years, in eight different houses in Milwaukee and Los Angeles, Otto lived secretly in the Osterreichs' attics.

On the fatal night, Otto said he was carrying a pistol in case of burglars, when he came upon Fred striking his wife. The two men tussled and the gun went off accidentally, killing Fred. The lovers decided to fake a burglary, and Otto locked Vally in her closet.

KILLER WIT
"Drama is life with the dull bits left out."
—ALFRED HITCHCOCK

No More Attics (Or, The Live-In Lover, Act II)

When we'd last seen Otto and Vally, they'd killed her husband and faked a robbery to cover it up.

Tired of living in attics, Otto hitched a ride to San Francisco several days after the murder with Vally's lawyer (and subsequent lover). There, Otto married and became manager of a hotel. Eight years later, the lawyer had a crisis of conscience when Vally ended their affair, and he turned her and Otto in to the police. The public seemed more amused than appalled by the story: Otto was sentenced to three years for manslaughter, but went free because of the statute of limitations. Charges against Vally were dropped when her trial ended in a hung jury.

Otto returned to his wife and his hotel suite. Vally opened a supermarket in Beverly Hills and lived in the "attic" above the store. Alone.

"Murder is born of love, and love attains the greatest intensity in murder."
—OCTAVE MIRBEAU

Losing Your Head over a Beautiful Woman

Beautiful women have been turning men's heads since the beginning of time, and a man who does something stupid while in lust is said to have "lost his head" over a woman.

Then there was Holofernes, commander-in-chief of the Assyrian army under Nebuchadnezzar. He was laying successful siege to the Israelite town of Bethulia, when who should wander into his camp but a beautiful, rich widow named Judith. She persuaded the smitten Holofernes that God was angry with the townspeople and would soon deliver them to defeat. If he would give her shelter in the camp and allow her out each day to pray, she would let him know when the time was ripe for attack.

After several days of "burning with the desire to possess her," Holofernes invited Judith to a banquet where she flirted with him and encouraged him to drink so heavily that he was passed out on his bed when all the servants finally left them alone. Then Holofernes truly lost his head over Judith—when she hacked it off with his own sword. She smuggled his head back to Bethulia, where it was displayed on the town wall to inspire the Israelites in battle. When the Assyrians realized Holofernes was dead, they fled in disarray.

> *"Not by youths was their mighty one struck down, nor did titans bring him low, nor huge giants attack him; But Judith, the daughter of Merari, By the beauty of her countenance disabled him."* —JUDITH 16:6, THE NEW AMERICAN BIBLE

Judy, Judy, Judy

Judith is a consistently popular name for girls in many countries.

You Can Never Have Enough Pseudonyms

Q: What's the real name of the bestselling author who wrote popular novels under the names Evan Hunter and Ed McBain—among others?

A: Salvatore A. Lombino, who was most widely recognized as the author of the most successful police procedural novels of all time, the immensely popular 87th Precinct series

Once upon a Murder

Edgar winner Ed McBain produced a very impressive legal series featuring Florida attorney Matthew Hope. The Hope series features fairy-tale titles such as:

- *Goldilocks* (1977)
- *Rumpelstiltskin* (1981)
- *Jack and the Beanstalk* (1984)
- *Cinderella* (1986)
- *Puss in Boots* (1987)
- *Three Blind Mice* (1990)
- *Mary, Mary* (1992)

> *"He sees death in the prostitutes who have witnessed the death of honor, and daily multiply the death of love, who bleed away their own lives fifty times a day beneath the relentless stabbings of countless conjugations."*
> —ED MCBAIN

Justice Is Just a Fairy Tale

Perhaps McBain's little joke in this title convention is that the criminal justice system is nothing but fantasy. The fairy-tale associations feature subtly in the novels. McBain's Matthew Hope (much like William G. Tapply's brilliant series character, Boston attorney Brady Coyne) isn't out to rid the world of murderers; they just seem to bump into him.

In *Rumpelstiltskin,* for example, Hope gets lucky and hooks up with a female '60s rock star for a lusty evening of sinful pleasure. Unfortunately, the aging rock star winds up brutally murdered.

Talk about getting screwed by a lawyer. Some things never change.

COP TALK: SEX, LIES, AND VIDEOTAPE

Sunny: *What does a girl have to do to go to bed with you?*
Harry Callahan: *Try knocking on the door.*
—CLINT EASTWOOD AS HARRY CALLAHAN AND ADELE YOSHIOKA AS
SUNNY IN *MAGNUM FORCE* (1973)

If You Can't Take a Cold Shower, Distract Yourself with These Police Thrillers

- *Blind Date* (1998) by Frances Fyfield
- *Dancing with the Virgins* (2001) by Stephen Booth
- *Faithless* (2005) by Karin Slaughter
- *The Girl of His Dreams* (2008) by Donna Leon
- *The Girls He Adored* (2001) by Jonathan Nasaw
- *Kiss the Girls* (1994) by James Patterson
- *The Last Temptation* (2002) by Val McDermid
- *Sex and Murder.Com* (2001) by Mark Richard Zubro
- *Sin City* (2002) by Max Allan Collins
- *The Stripper* (1961) by Carter Brown

⚲ *First Lines*

"The Rand Brothers Mortuary was so beautiful it almost made you want to die." —*DIG THAT CRAZY GRAVE* (1961) BY RICHARD S. PRATHER

P.Eye Candy for Him

- Anne Francis as Honey West (*Honey West*, 1965–1966)
- Farrah Fawcett as Jill Munroe (*Charlie's Angels*, 1976–1977; 1978–1980)
- Kate Jackson as Sabrina Duncan (*Charlie's Angels*, 1976–1979)
- Jaclyn Smith as Kelly Garrett (*Charlie's Angels*, 1976–1981)
- Cheryl Ladd as Kris Munroe (*Charlie's Angels*, 1977–1981)
- Shelley Hack as Tiffany Welles (*Charlie's Angels*, 1979–1980)

- Tanya Roberts as Julie Rogers (*Charlie's Angels*, 1980–1981)
- Stephanie Zimbalist as Laura Holt (*Remington Steele*, 1982–1987)
- Cybill Shepherd as Madelyn "Maddie" Hayes (*Moonlighting*, 1985–1989)

KILLER WIT

"My dear, you're sitting on your best profile."

—ALFRED HITCHCOCK, TO THE ACTRESS WHO ASKED HIM IF HER RIGHT OR LEFT PROFILE WAS BETTER

Lone Wolf P.I.s More Comfortable with a Mate

While some fictional private investigators have managed to keep a relationship going, most are single due to their dark outlooks on life, or just the stresses and schedule of the job. Some (think Sam Spade and Brigid O'Shaughnessy) have even turned in their love interests!

Match the P.I.s and their significant others with their creators:

1. Nick and Nora Charles

2. Brock Callahan and Jan Bonnett

3. Ben Helm and Greta Murdock

4. Paul and Maureen Shaw

5. Ellen and Carney Wilde

6. Johnny and Suzy Marshall

7. Quin St. James and Mike McCleary

8. Pete and Jeannie Schoefield

9. Jim and Sandy Bennett

10. Michael and Phyllis Shayne

a. Bart Spicer

b. Bruno Fischer

c. Robert Martin

d. T. J. MacGregor

e. William C. Gault

f. Thomas B. Dewey

g. Mark Sadler

h. Brett Halliday

i. James M. Fox

j. Dashiell Hammett

ANSWERS: 1-j; 2-e; 3-b; 4-g; 5-a; 6-i; 7-d; 8-f; 9-c; 10-h

✑ *First Lines*

"Even though I was in my office trying to recuperate from an ill-fated relationship, my digits trailed along the hall, descended the building's stairwell, and meandered up and down every dark alley in the world. I was non-terminating, non-repeating. I was Pi, the private eye, the rational irrational. And Rachel used to make me feel special."—"PI, P.I." (2010) BY STEPHEN D. ROGERS

The Quotable P.I. ─────────────────────

Harry Orwell: *How old are you?*

Girl Clerk: *I'm twenty . . . almost twenty-one.*

Harry Orwell: *Ever go fishing?*

Girl Clerk: *I'd love to!*

Harry Orwell: *Sometimes when you go fishing you catch a little fish. You have to let them go and throw them back . . . 'cause they're too young.*

Girl Clerk: *Do you really have to let them go?*

Harry Orwell: *Yes. It's a pity.*

—DAVID JANSSEN AS HARRY ORWELL IN *HARRY O* (1974–1976)

✑ *First Lines*

"The first time he saw her, he simply knew." —*THE PERFECT HUSBAND* (1997) BY LISA GARDNER

Stranger Than Fiction

Q: What real-life lethal couple inspired James M. Cain's novella and the subsequent movie, *Double Indemnity*?

A: In 1927, an attractive blonde housewife from Long Island and her lover, a married corset salesman, were tried for the murder of her husband. The prosecution contended that Ruth Brown Snyder and Henry Judd Gray conspired to kill art director Albert Snyder while he slept and make the crime look like a burglary gone bad. Mrs. Snyder, the state claimed, had taken out a $53,000 life insurance policy on her husband without his knowledge, a policy that paid double the amount in case of accidental death. In court, the lovers each blamed the other for Snyder's death. They were both convicted and executed in the electric chair.

⌘ *First Lines*

"After nearly a quarter of a century of marriage, Richie Meyers, my husband, told me to call him Rick." —*AFTER ALL THESE YEARS* (1993) BY SUSAN ISAACS

DEADLY DIALOGUE

Dooley: *All right, let's get one thing straight: The woman is mine! Now we're both members of the animal kingdom. You know that and I know that. And we both know that this thing is really primal.*

—JAMES BELUSHI AS DETECTIVE MIKE DOOLEY IN *K-9* (1989)

Bible Bedtime Stories: Levite Swap

A Levite and his concubine passed through a village while traveling and sought shelter with a friendly man and his family. Many of the villagers wanted to rape the Levite, but his host was determined to protect his guest. The man offered his own daughter instead, but the villagers refused. So the Levite pushed his concubine outside. In the morning, the Levite found his concubine at the doorstep. He told her to get up, but she was dead as a doornail.

"Blondes make the best victims. They're like virgin snow that shows up the bloody footprints." —ALFRED HITCHCOCK

The Hitchcock Blonde

Genius director Alfred Hitchcock loved his leading ladies—and he loved them blonde. Match the actress to the Hitchcock film in which she starred.

1. Tippi Hedren	**a.** *I Confess* (1953)
2. Eva Marie Saint	**b.** *North by Northwest* (1959)
3. Grace Kelly	**c.** *Saboteur* (1942)
4. Doris Day	**d.** *Notorious* (1946)
5. Ingrid Bergman	**e.** *Stage Fright* (1950)
6. Kim Novak	**f.** *Marnie* (1964)
7. Janet Leigh	**g.** *Vertigo* (1958)
8. Madeleine Carroll	**h.** *Rear Window* (1954)
9. Priscilla Lane	**i.** *The 39 Steps* (1935)
10. Anne Baxter	**j.** *The Man Who Knew Too Much* (1956)
11. Marlene Dietrich	**k.** *Psycho* (1960)

ANSWERS: 1-f; 2-b; 3-h, 4-j; 5-d; 6-g; 7-k; 8-i; 9-c; 10-a; 11-e

> *"In my experience, I know of five cases of wives being murdered by their devoted husbands."* —HERCULE POIROT IN *AGATHA CHRISTIE'S POIROT:* "THE DOUBLE CLUE" (1991)

Lusting for the Ladies

Many a woman's body has lured a man into murder. That's true in life and, especially, in movies. The film *Body Heat* comes readily to mind, as does *The Postman Always Rings Twice*, both versions (all based on books by James M. Cain). And, oh, maybe quite a few thousand other flicks.

DEADLY DIALOGUE

Cora: *I'm getting tired of what's right and wrong.*
Frank Chambers: *They hang people for that, Cora!*
—JACK NICHOLSON AS FRANK CHAMBERS AND JESSICA LANGE AS
CORA IN *THE POSTMAN ALWAYS RINGS TWICE* (1981)

Stranger Than Fiction

Q: What true-crime case inspired Joyce Carol Oates's award-winning story about the turmoil of adolescence, "Where Are You Going, Where Have You Been?"
A: Charles Schmid, the so-called "Pied Piper of Tucson," killed three teenage girls and left their bodies in the desert. Oates's story was also the basis for the movie *Smooth Talk*, which won a Grand Jury Award at the 1986 Sundance Festival.

Smooth Criminal

The twenty-three-year-old Charles "Smitty" Schmid was an older, charismatic figure to bored Tucson teens hanging out on the Speedway strip. He spun wild stories about himself to gain admiration or sympathy, spent lavishly on parties, and indulged his passions for sex and rock 'n' roll. In May 1964, Schmid and his girlfriend lured Alleen Rowe, age fifteen, out to the desert, where he killed her just to see what it felt like. A year later he strangled another girlfriend, Gretchen Fritz, age seventeen, and her thirteen-year-old sister, Wendy. He confided his crimes to one of his hangers-on, who later went to the police when he feared Schmid might target his girlfriend next. Schmid was stabbed to death in prison in 1975.

> *"What seemed to intrigue people most about Smitty—girls and boys alike—was his freedom. He did whatever he wanted and his daredevil ways made him seem larger than life."* —KATHERINE RAMSLAND, "CHARLES SCHMID: THE PIED PIPER" (2006)

*** First Lines**

"In Southern New Hampshire there is a road that some call Death Highway." — *TEACH ME TO KILL* (1991) BY STEPHEN SAWICKI

Pre-Nups and Perpetuities = Murder

Legal crime stories often turn on obscure points of law. Like the ones in *Body Heat*, the sizzling 1981 remake of *Double Indemnity*, written and directed by Lawrence Kasdan. The sexy, voluptuous Mrs. Matty Walker (Kathleen Turner) uses lust as the lure and greed as the motive to ensnare inept attorney Ned Racine (William Hurt) in her pernicious plot. Matty wants her husband, Edmund Walker (Richard Crenna), dead and she's willing to use her body and charm to get the job done. She convinces her "kept" man, Racine, to do the deed, but not before he recommends divorce.

> *"Lust is what keeps you wanting to do it even when you have no desire to be with each other. Love is what makes you want to be with each other even when you have no desire to do it."* —JUDITH VIORST

First, the Pre-Nup

Unfortunately, a prenuptial agreement stands between Mrs. Matty Walker of *Body Heat* and millions. It must be murder, but even this solution is not without problems. Edmund will leave half of his estate to his niece, and greedy Matty wants it all. So prior to the murder she forges a new will and makes it appear to have been drafted by Racine. To throw off suspicion, Matty leaves in the provision bequeathing half the estate to Edmund's niece.

> *"Well, some men, once they get a whiff of it, they trail you like a hound."*
> —KATHLEEN TURNER AS MATTY WALKER IN *BODY HEAT* (1981)

Next, the Perp

Notwithstanding, cunning Matty finds a way to manipulate Racine's reputation as an inept lawyer. She drafts the will in violation of the obscure common law Rule Against Perpetuities—essentially, the gift to Edmund's niece won't vest within the time period required by the obscure rule. Edmund's "new" will is null and void and as a result he is considered to have died without a will. Matty, as his spouse, gets the whole ball of wax and Racine gets a personal introduction to the criminal justice system he won't soon forget. The moral of the story: Where there's a will, there's a way around it.

The Quotable P.I.

Continental Op: *You think I'm a man and you're a woman. That's wrong. I'm a manhunter and you're something that has been running in front of me. There's nothing human about it.*
—THE CONTINENTAL OP IN "THE GUTTING OF COUFFIGNAL" (1925)
BY DASHIELL HAMMETT

Turning the Heat Up on Kathleen Turner

With some of the sexiest love scenes on film, *Body Heat* launched Turner's career and earned her a spot on *Empire* magazine's list of sexiest stars in film history. Full of legal twists and love twists, *Body Heat* is a superb study of how lust and greed are used to manipulate and serve amoral people of design.

DEADLY DIALOGUE

Alex: *What are we gonna do? Talk about me sex life?*
Psychiatrist: *Oh, no. I'm going to show you some slides and you're going to tell me what you think about them. Alright?*
—MALCOLM MCDOWELL AS ALEX AND PAULINE TAYLOR AS THE PSYCHIATRIST IN *A CLOCKWORK ORANGE* (1971)

Phallic Weapons on Film

One of the more unusual weapons used in a cinematic attack was an homage to a crucial part of a man's body: the giant penis statue from *A Clockwork Orange*. Alex used it to fend off and then batter a woman when he invaded her home. In Guy Ritchie's film, *Lock, Stock and Two Smoking Barrels*, in a clear case of some kind of envy, there was the somewhat smaller black rubber dildo, which, as Bacon explains, Hatchet Harry used to collect on a debt.

"Harry didn't think that he did a very good job, so he grabbed the nearest thing to hand, which just so happened to be a fifteen-inch black rubber cock, and proceeded to beat poor old Smithy to death with. And that was seen as a nice way to go. Now that is why you pay Hatchet Harry when you owe." —JASON STATHAM AS BACON IN *LOCK, STOCK AND TWO SMOKING BARRELS* (1998)

The Vagina Murderers

To even the gender score, however, there's the vagina (yes, vagina) in *Lady Terminator* (1989), an Indonesian ripoff of *The Terminator*, and Chesty Morgan's breasts in *Double Agent 73* (1974). Cheesy, but true.

COP TALK: SEX, LIES, AND VIDEOTAPE

Mike: *What, you got laid last night?*

Mad Dog: *I don't get laid, I make love.*

—ROBERT DE NIRO AS OFFICER WAYNE "MAD DOG" DOBIE AND DAVID CARUSO AS MIKE IN *MAD DOG AND GLORY* (1993)

Sate Your (Wander) Lust

Here's the perfect reading list for poor armchair travelers:

- Christopher G. Moore hires Vincent "Vinee" Calvino to take you on a tour of Thailand, starting with *Spirit House* (2004).
- Tarquin Hall hires Vish Puri to take you on a tour of India, starting with *The Case of the Missing Servant* (2009).
- Diane Wei Liang hires Wang Mei to take you on a tour of China, starting with *The Eye of Jade* (2007).
- Peter Tasker hires Kazuo Mori to take you on a tour of Japan, starting with *Silent Thunder* (1992).
- Peter Corris hires Cliff Hardy to take you on a tour of Australia, starting with *The Dying Trade* (1980).
- Paul Johnston hires Alex Mavros to take you on a tour of Greece, starting with *A Deeper Shade of Blue* (2002).
- Cara Black hires Aimée Léduc to take you on a tour of France, starting with *Murder in the Marais* (1998).
- Manuel Vazquez Montalban hires Pepe Carvalho to take you on a tour of Spain, starting with *Yo Mate a Kennedy* (1972).
- Jassy Mackenzie hires Jade de Jong to take you on a tour of South Africa, starting with *Random Violence* (2008).
- Paco Ignacio Taibo II hires Héctor Belascoarán Shayne to take you on a tour of Mexico, starting with *An Easy Thing* (1990).

> *"That is my ambition, to have killed more people—more helpless people —than any man or woman who has ever lived."* —JANE TOPPAN

KILLER WIT

"I don't know if this is a matter for the costume department or the hairdresser."

—ALFRED HITCHCOCK, IN ANSWER TO THE CREW COMPLAINTS THAT TALLULAH BANKHEAD'S HABIT OF NOT WEARING UNDERPANTS WAS CREATING CAMERA ANGLE PROBLEMS IN SHOOTING LIFEBOAT

Jealousy and Lust on the (Michiganian) Peninsula

Q: What is the best trial movie ever made?

A: More than half a century later, this description of *Anatomy of a Murder* (1959) still holds true.

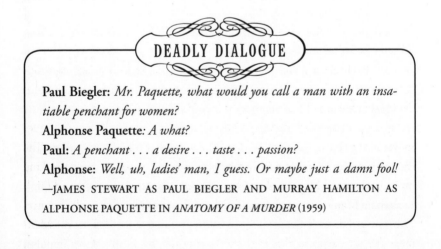

DEADLY DIALOGUE

Paul Biegler: *Mr. Paquette, what would you call a man with an insatiable penchant for women?*

Alphonse Paquette: *A what?*

Paul: *A penchant . . . a desire . . . taste . . . passion?*

Alphonse: *Well, uh, ladies' man, I guess. Or maybe just a damn fool!*

—JAMES STEWART AS PAUL BIEGLER AND MURRAY HAMILTON AS ALPHONSE PAQUETTE IN *ANATOMY OF A MURDER* (1959)

Origins of a Legend

Q: On which work was *Anatomy of a Murder* based?

A: The movie was based on the 1958 number-one bestseller by Michigan Supreme Court Justice John D. Voelker under the *nom de plume* Robert Traver. Voelker based the novel on a 1952 case in which he served as defense counsel. The central character is former DA Paul Biegler (James Stewart) who would rather spend his time fishing and swapping lies with his chum Parnell McCarthy (Arthur O'Connell), an old sot and washed-up lawyer. Biegler hangs up his waders when the gorgeous and all-too-flirtatious Laura Manion (Lee Remick) shows up at his small-town law office to retain him to defend her husband, U.S. Army Lieutenant Frederick Manion (Ben Gazzara), who's been charged with murder. Laura was purportedly raped by a lust-driven lowlife innkeeper and when the angry, short-tempered Frederick finds out, he kills him.

A Judicious Cameo

A wonderful, authentic touch to *Anatomy of a Murder*: The presiding judge is played by Joseph N. Welch, who made some fame as an attorney when he upbraided Senator Joseph McCarthy.

The Irresistible Impulse Defense

As the drama of *Anatomy of a Murder* builds, Biegler devises an ingenious defense based on irresistible impulse. The courtroom scenes are tense and brilliantly constructed, discussing (to the shock of some audience members) the realities of rape and how victims are often put on trial. James Stewart as Biegler moves in the courtroom with an ease Daniel Webster might have envied. The legal debates and erudite jabs between Biegler and the high-profile-seeking prosecutor named Dancer, played by George C. Scott, are so real you'd think Lieutenant Manion was actually on trial and Dancer's job hung in the balance. The movie ends with Beigler and McCarthy reading a note left by the Manions. The note explains that they were compelled, by an irresistible impulse, to stiff Biegler on his fee, leaving the viewer to wonder if Frederick really was compelled to commit the murder by an irresistible impulse or jealousy.

> *"I've looked on many women with lust. I've committed adultery in my heart many times. God knows I will do this and forgives me."* —JIMMY CARTER

Calling All Barristers

Sir John Mortimer, creator of the much-loved *Rumpole of the Bailey* novels and BBC series, was in real life as irritable, lovable, wild, and witty as his English barrister alter ego. And he was likewise no English prig. Not by a long shot. Prior to the enormous success of his *Rumpole of the Bailey* series and before earning the coveted title "Sir," Mortimer was a well-accomplished barrister who had a gift for winning difficult cases.

Bollocks! It's the Sex Pistols!

One of his most famous cases concerned an obscenity charge brought against the notorious English punk rock band the Sex Pistols. The Sex Pistols had been handed the obscenity charge for releasing an album called *Never Mind the Bollocks*. Mortimer took on the case and argued that the word "bollocks" was in fact not offensive and further, that the harmless word had been singled out as offensive by the testy Brits simply because the Sex Pistols placed it on their album cover.

Mortimer on the White Wig

> *"If you are about to be sent down for life, you don't want someone in a T-shirt, jeans, and trainers doing it. You want the whole works."* —SIR JOHN MORTIMER, AUTHOR AND BARRISTER

The Chaucer Defense

Ever the scholar, Mortimer pointed out to the court that the word had been used as far back as the Bible, Chaucer, and even George Orwell. Thanks to Mortimer's well-rounded argument, the Sex Pistol's use of "bollocks" was upheld. Perhaps the presiding chairman feared there'd be a hung jury.

You're the Boss of Me

Q: What does character Horace Rumpole call his formidable wife, Hilda?

A: She Who Must Be Obeyed

> *"I never plead guilty."* —HORACE RUMPOLE OF *RUMPOLE OF THE BAILEY* (1978–1992)

Bible Bedtime Stories: Pegged!

Sisera was a defeated general who escaped his final battle and hid in the tent of a woman named Jael who favored the Israelites. She offered him milk and a cot to sleep on and, while he slept, she drove a tent peg through his skull.

✑ First Lines

"Love, although the staple diet of the Oxford Book of English Verse, *and the subject which seems the concern of the majority of its contributors, has not, so far much disturbed the even course of these memoirs, which have mainly been concerned with bloodstains, mayhem, murder, and other such signs of affection."* —"RUMPOLE AND THE COURSE OF TRUE LOVE" (1979) BY JOHN MORTIMER

The Rape That Wasn't

In 1999, when DNA from three rape victims matched his with a probability of three trillion to one, Anthony Turner was convicted of rape. Turner claimed the DNA must have come from someone else, but he had no twin brother. While he was awaiting sentencing, a woman said she had been raped. When tested, her attacker's DNA matched Turner's—even though he had been in jail at the time of the last rape. Impossible? Not as much as you might think.

As it turns out, the woman who made the fourth (and final) accusation had been hired by members of Turner's family. They paid her $50 to make the rape claim, and even supplied her with "evidence"—all to discredit the three previous, positive DNA tests. The semen that had been tested had actually been snuck out of prison by Turner in a ketchup packet.

Lusting for Some Great P.I. Fiction?

- *Kiss Me, Deadly* (1952) by Mickey Spillane
- *Sleep with Strangers* (1955) by Dolores Hitchens
- *Strip for Murder* (1956) by Richard S. Prather
- *Sleeping Beauty* (1973) by Ross MacDonald
- *The Last Good Kiss* (1978) by James Crumley
- *Skinflick* (1979) by Joseph Hansen
- *Kiss* (1988) by John Lutz

- *Devil in a Blue Dress* (1990) by Walter Mosley
- *Dancing in the Dark* (1996) by Stuart M. Kaminsky
- *Angel in Black* (2001) by Max Allan Collins

Trial by Infatuated Jury

In 1905, when only men could serve, two juries deadlocked on whether pretty brunette dancer Nan Patterson shot Caesar Young to death while riding alone with him in a hansom cab. It seems Nan was trying to hold on to her rich and once-ardent lover, but Young had reconciled with his wife and was sailing for Europe with her later that day. He had clearly and publicly rejected Nan, and yet, she claimed, Young must have had a sudden fit of despondency and shot himself in the chest. (He then, apparently, tucked the pistol back into his coat pocket.) Nan maintained she hadn't actually seen the shooting because she was gazing out the window at the time.

Her defense counsel asked if the jury could believe that "this empty—frivolous, if you like—pleasure-loving girl" could invent such a story. The "infatuated jury," wrote *New Yorker* correspondent Alexander Woollcott—just like "the susceptible twelve" before them—could not agree that such a thing had happened, and Nan Patterson went free.

> *"The mistress has lost, lost her handsome, generous lover. . . . A little crack, a little puff of smoke, a dead man prostrate on a woman's knee, the wages of sin were paid!"* —PROSECUTOR WILLIAM RAND AT NAN PATTERSON'S TRIAL

A Blonde by Any Other Name

Name ten crime novels with "blond" or "blonde" in the title.

- *The Blond Baboon* (1978) by Janwillem van de Wetering
- *Blond Run* (2009) by Jim Michael Hansen
- *Blonde Faith* (2007) by Walter Mosley
- *Blondes Have More Felons* (2006) by Alesia Holliday
- *The Case of the Blonde Bonanza* (Perry Mason) (1962) by Erle Stanley Gardner
- *Chasing a Blond Moon* (2003) by Joseph Heywood
- *The Concrete Blonde* (1994) by Michael Connelly
- *Dirty Blonde* (2006) by Lisa Scottoline
- *Lethally Blond* (2007) by Kate White
- *The Shimmering Blond Sister* (2010) by David Handler

"Murders are exciting and lift people into a heart-beating awe as religion is supposed to do, after seeing one in the street young couples will go back to bed and make love, people will cross themselves and thank God for the gift of their stuporous lives, old folks will talk to each other over cups of hot water with lemon because murders are enlivened sermons to be analyzed and considered and relished, they speak to the timid of the dangers of rebellion, murders are perceived as momentary descents of God and so provide joy and hope and righteous satisfaction to parishioners, who will talk about them for years afterward to anyone who will listen."
—E. L. DOCTOROW

Partners in Lust after a Martini

Q: What happens when you get caught lusting it up with the boss's wife? And your boss happens to be a partner in the swish law firm where you work?

A: You get canned and become attorney Steve Martini's central character, corporate-turned–criminal lawyer Paul Madriani.

> **Martini**
>
> n.: 1. a classic cocktail comprised of gin or vodka enhanced with bitters and a twist.
>
> 2. *Steve*—an American attorney and novelist who composes legal thrillers—with many twists.

That's Martini's Madriani

Paul Madriani first appears in *Compelling Evidence* (1992), and readers not previously bitten by the legal thriller bug soon felt Martini's sting. In *Compelling Evidence*, Madriani is conned into representing his former mistress, Talia Potter, for the murder of her husband, Ben Potter—the law partner who fired Madriani a year ago! Now Potter's greedy former partner, Tony "The Greek" Skarpellos, could cash in on some major bank if Madriani botches Talia's defense.

Courtroom Drama at Its Finest

Martini's excellent characterizations, combined with his superb talent for legal intrigue, produce some of the best modern courtroom thrillers in the genre. A background in legal journalism and, of course, law make for excellent plot structure in the Martini canon:

- *Prime Witness* (1993)
- *Undue Influence* (1994)
- *The Judge* (1996)
- *The Attorney* (1999)
- *The Jury* (2001)
- *The Arraignment* (2003)
- *Double Tap* (2006)
- *Shadow of Power* (2008)

- *Guardian of Lies* (2009)
- *The Rule of Nine* (2010)

She Always Gets Her Murderer

Match the actress with the movie in which she always gets her man, uh, murderer.

1. *Suspect* (1987)
2. *Silence of the Lambs* (1991)
3. *V.I. Warshawski* (1991)
4. *Fargo* (1996)
5. *Miss Congeniality* (2000)
6. *The Big Easy* (1986)
7. *Lara Croft: Tomb Raider* (2001)
8. *Red* (2010)

a. Frances McDormand
b. Angelina Jolie
c. Cher
d. Helen Mirren
e. Kathleen Turner
f. Ellen Barkin
g. Jodie Foster
h. Sandra Bullock

ANSWERS: 1-c; 2-g; 3-e; 4-a; 5-h; 6-f; 7-b; 8-d

Lust, Law, and Finally—Ladies!

Q: What popular television series, created by David E. Kelley, made short shrift—and short skirts—out of the legal profession?

A: *Ally McBeal,* brainchild of the creator of such blockbuster legal programs as *The Practice* and *Boston Legal*, was an ingenious retort to the male-dominated genre. From 1997 until 2002, the hugely successful American legal comedy-drama, *Ally McBeal,* entertained audiences, with Calista Flockhart playing its eponymous main character.

Sex in the Courtroom

Ally McBeal proved itself endlessly inventive. Set at the fictional Boston law firm of Cage & Fish, a highly sexualized environment played the backdrop—and in many episodes was forefront to the case at bar. The show often focused on how social issues affect law or the law affects social issues. In any event, Ally's romantic interests and eccentricities dictated her day-to-day grind as an attorney and vice-versa.

> *"Whenever I get depressed, I raise my hemlines. If things don't change, I am bound to be arrested."* —CALISTA FLOCKHART AS ALLY MCBEAL

The Shorter, the Better

McBeal, despite protests from feminist and professional women who took umbrage at her short skirts, has become somewhat of a cult figure to many women entering legal and professional scenes. And much to her fans' delight, after some—you guessed it—legal issues, the show finally became available on DVD in 2009.

A Lustful Sensation

Q: Who was one of the leading authors of the so-called sensation novels of the nineteenth century, precursors to today's crime novels?

A: Although not necessarily recognized as a barrister-writer, Wilkie Collins (mostly remembered for his 1868 novel *The Moonstone*) certainly did his share of mixing law and "sin" into his literary works. And while his writing style may be old hat, the social issues he discusses in his works seem like they are ripped right from Fox News.

Match the social issue to the Wilkie Collins novel:

1. *No Name* (1862)
2. *Armadale* (1866)
3. *Evil Genius* (1886)

a. Prostitution and abortion
b. Divorce and custody disputes
c. The rights of illegitimate children

ANSWERS: 1-c; 2-b; 3-a

What If . . .

Collins's ability to address some of the most heated debates of his time makes one think that, were he writing today, illegal immigration, hanging chads, and adulterous politicians would be on his hit list. Now where's the sin in that?

Fickle Finger-Pointing of Fate

In 1911, an affluent Virginia man named Henry Beattie Jr. said he, his wife, Louise, and their infant son were attacked by a highwayman who shot Louise point-blank and somehow missed Henry completely. Turns out Beattie had bought the murder weapon, the blood spatter didn't match his story, and his mistress may have been pressuring him to marry her.

The Quotable P.I. ———————————————

Philip Marlowe: *She'd make a jazzy weekend, but she'd be a bit wearing for a steady diet.* —ROBERT MITCHUM AS PHILIP MARLOWE IN *THE BIG SLEEP* (1978)

Lust, Violence, and the Real McCoy

Q: Which female New York prosecutor writes international bestsellers featuring Special Victims Unit Assistant DA Alexandra "Alex" Cooper?

A: Linda Fairstein is considered one of America's foremost prosecutors in connection with crimes of sexual assault and domestic violence, having run the Sex Crimes Unit of the District Attorney's Office in Manhattan for more than twenty years. With the 1996 release of her highly acclaimed first novel, *Final Jeopardy*, Fairstein introduced the unflappable Cooper, who—like Fairstein—knows how to crack a case.

Alex Makes the Case

The *New York Times*–bestselling Cooper canon is fast-paced and action-packed:

- *Likely to Die* (1997)
- *Cold Hit* (1999)
- *The Deadhouse* (2001)
- *The Bone Vault* (2003)
- *The Kills* (2004)
- *Entombed* (2005)
- *Death Dance* (2006)
- *Bad Blood* (2007)
- *Killer Heat* (2008)
- *Lethal Legacy* (2009)
- *Hell Gate* (2010)
- *Silent Mercy* (2011)

GLUTTONY

n., from the Latin *gutire*, to swallow

1. Eating or drinking to excess
2. The act or practice of eating to excess
3. Overindulgence in something; voraciousness

"The flesh endures the storms of the present alone; the mind, those of the past and future as well as the present. Gluttony is a lust of the mind."
—**THOMAS HOBBES**

Gluttons are addicted to food, booze, drugs, sex—even punishment. Stand in the way between a glutton and that addiction, and you could find yourself under fire—or six feet under.

> *"The greatest crimes are caused by surfeit, not by want."* —ARISTOTLE,
> *POLITICS*

Dinner Is Murder

Ten films in which food and drink and death are all on the menu:

1. *301/302* (1995)
2. *Arsenic and Old Lace* (1944)
3. *The Cook, the Thief, His Wife, and Her Lover* (1989)
4. *Eating Raoul* (1982)
5. *Frenzy* (1972)
6. *Fried Green Tomatoes* (1991)
7. *Prime Cut* (1972)
8. *Scotland, Pa* (2001)
9. *Titus* (1999)
10. *Who Is Killing the Great Chefs of Europe?* (1978)

> *"Murder is commoner among cooks than among members of any other*
> *profession."* —W. H. AUDEN

The Quotable P.I.

Harry Angel: *I gotta thing about chickens.* —MICKEY ROURKE AS P.I.
HARRY ANGEL IN *ANGEL HEART* (1987)

COP TALK: DONUTS AND MORE

Martin Riggs: *Do you like your chili with or without crushed Oreos?*
—MEL GIBSON AS SERGEANT MARTIN RIGGS IN *LETHAL WEAPON 2*
(1989)

You're Too Fat When . . .

If he hadn't been dead, King Eglon of the Moabites would have been so embarrassed by certain details of his assassination (Judges 3:12–30). It seems Eglon had been collecting tribute from the defeated Israelites for eighteen years and had grown immensely fat. Finally, the fed-up Israelites sent their next shipment of tribute by way of Ehud ben-Gera, who also brought along a double-edged sword about eighteen inches long. Ehud was known to be left-handed, so King Eglon's bodyguards overlooked the sword he had hidden along his right thigh.

After Ehud had turned over the money and goods sent in tribute, he persuaded King Eglon to meet with him alone to hear a "secret message." Eglon sent all his attendants away and met with Ehud in his private rooms. "I have a message for you from God," said Ehud, and he delivered it with a sword thrust into Eglon's immense belly.

> *"Even the handle sank in after the blade, and his bowels discharged. Ehud did not pull the sword out, and the fat closed in over it."* —JUDGES 3:22 NIV

A Glutton's Demise

Yuck. Eglon's servants returned to find his door locked and assumed, as must have often been the case, that the king was detained in his "throne room." After an embarrassingly long interval, they broke down the door and found Eglon dead and leaking, with rolls of fat engulfing the handle of the sword. Ehud, meanwhile, slipped away to raise an army that defeated the Moabites, and he reigned over Israel as one of the great judges.

Named for a Murderer
Ehud is a popular name for boys in Israel.

COP TALK: MAD AS HELL
Harry Callahan: *May I make a statement, McKay?*
Captain McKay: *Go ahead!*
Harry Callahan: *Your mouthwash ain't makin' it.*
—CLINT EASTWOOD AS INSPECTOR "DIRTY" HARRY CALLAHAN AND
BRADFORD DILLMAN AS CAPTAIN MCKAY IN *THE ENFORCER* (1976)

COP TALK: DONUTS AND MORE
Sonny Crockett: *Man, it's so hot you could fry an egg on my face.*
Ricardo Tubbs: *Hope I never get that hungry.*
—DON JOHNSON AS DETECTIVE JAMES "SONNY" CROCKETT AND
PHILIP MICHAEL THOMAS AS DETECTIVE RICARDO TUBBS IN *MIAMI
VICE* (1984–1990)

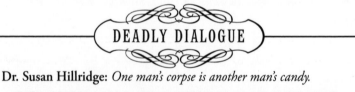

DEADLY DIALOGUE

Dr. Susan Hillridge: *One man's corpse is another man's candy.*
—ALICIA COPPOLA AS DR. SUSAN HILLRIDGE IN *CSI: CRIME SCENE
INVESTIGATION* (2000–)

Scratch-and-Sniff Book—Not!
Your CSI Lab at Work: Get the Real Scents of What It's Like in a Forensics Lab

Lose the Weight, Not the Wife

Celebrity chef Juan-Carlos Cruz, having lost forty-three pounds, tried to lose about 120 pounds more—his wife. Cruz is a 1993 graduate of the California Culinary Academy. As a pastry chef at the Hotel Bel-Air in Los Angeles, he created delectable treats for such celebrities as Jack Nicholson, Oprah Winfrey, and Julia Roberts. Too much sampling, however, had Cruz looking like the Pillsbury Doughboy. He enrolled in the *Discovery Health Body Challenge 3* on cable TV, lost a lot of weight, and gained his own Food Network show, *Calorie Commando.*

In May 2010, Cruz, then age forty-eight, was arrested for trying to hire three homeless men to kill his wife, attorney Jennifer Campbell. The couple had been sweet on each other since high school, but he, at least, had soured on the romance. (When Jennifer found out, she must have been frosted.) Lucky for her, the prospective hit men found Cruz's offer not to their taste and contacted the cops. Cruz ended up starring in a police video production, *The Chef Is Toast.* He was sentenced to nine years in prison, where he can work in the kitchen whipping up aphrodisiac dishes for the other inmates from his new cookbook—this is true—*The Love Diet.*

> *"It seems that whatever we do is somehow beyond reproach—murder, rape, drunk driving—as long as we go on a TV show and apologize."*
> —ERIC STOLTZ

✑ *First Lines*

"This was a party that Cholly Knickerbocker, in tomorrow's Los Angeles Examiner, would describe as 'a gathering of the Smart Set,' and if this was the Smart Set I was glad I belonged to the Stupid Set." —*STRIP FOR MURDER* (1955) BY RICHARD S. PRATHER

COP TALK: DONUTS AND MORE

Inspector Cobb: *Have you been drinking, McClane?*

John McClane: *No, not since this morning.*

—BRUCE WILLIS AS DETECTIVE JOHN MCCLANE AND LARRY BRYGGMAN AS INSPECTOR WALTER COBB IN *DIE HARD: WITH A VENGEANCE* (1995)

The Quotable P.I. _____

Honey West: *That fat man who came to my apartment isn't exactly the kind everybody loves.*

Ben Fancher: *Fat man? You saw the Fat Man?*

Honey West: *Every pound.*

—ANNE FRANCIS AS P.I. HONEY WEST AND NORMAN ALDEN AS BEN FANCHER IN *HONEY WEST* (1965–1966)

Are You Feeling Lucky?

Then name the Dirty Harry movie from which the following dialogue is drawn:

Harry Callahan: Oh, you can set yourself into a bonfire, we'll break out the marshmallows and the weenies, but you ain't gonna be on "News at Eleven."

ANSWER: *The Dead Pool* (1988)

First Lines

"August 30th is National Toasted Marshmallow Day, so, naturally, we're celebrating.

"Sure there's some debate. Is National Toasted Marshmallow Day August 14th or August 30th? We go with the 30th because it's closer to Labor

Day. Besides, if you dig a little deeper, you'll discover that August 14th is also National Creamsicle Day, and we firmly believe Creamsicles deserve their own separate day of national recognition." —MAD MOUSE (2006) BY
CHRIS GRABENSTEIN

Hollywood Lust (or, The "Fatty" Arbuckle Case)

If ever there was a Hollywood case that made headlines and ruined lives, it was the rape/murder case against Roscoe "Fatty" Arbuckle. A silent movie comedian second in popularity only to Charlie Chaplin, Arbuckle was accused of raping aspiring actress Virginia Rappe during a party at a San Francisco hotel in 1921. She had accompanied him into a bedroom during the party. Later, she was heard to cry out, "He hurt me!" and "He did it!" She was not hospitalized until two days later and died as a result of a ruptured bladder. Her friend, Bambina Delmont, told police that Arbuckle had raped Rappe. It was theorized that Arbuckle's heavy weight on her may have led to the rupture of Rappe's bladder. Luckily for Arbuckle, the case rested on dubious and shifting testimony from a few party guests and medical witnesses. The woman who made the rape charge never testified, perhaps because of her record for extortion, bigamy, fraud, and racketeering. After two deadlocked juries and plausible claims of prosecutorial misconduct, Arbuckle was swiftly acquitted in a third trial.

"Acquittal is not enough for Roscoe Arbuckle. We feel that a great injustice has been done to him . . . there was not the slightest proof adduced to connect him in any way with the commission of a crime. He was manly throughout the case and told a straightforward story which we all believe. We wish him success and hope that the American people will take the judgment of fourteen men and women that Roscoe Arbuckle is entirely innocent and free from all blame." —FOREMAN OF THE JURY
THAT ACQUITTED ARBUCKLE

Not Exactly an Ingénue in White

Though portrayed by the prosecution as an innocent, Rappe was a thirty-year-old who had undergone a number of abortions in the years previous to her death—any one of which could have done lasting damage to her internal organs. She also drank excessively and, since alcohol was also illegal, no one could ever be sure what exactly was in bootleg hootch. There's no telling exactly what damage had been done to her body before that fated hotel party.

Innocence Is Not Enough

Acquittal may not have been good enough for a jury that thought Arbuckle innocent, but for the American public—who believed far less of him—it was far from enough to end the scandal and re-establish his reputation. Rumors about what had gone on at the party, especially between Arbuckle and Rappe, spelled disaster for his cinema career. Fatty Arbuckle returned to movies as a director and briefly as a featured performer. He died of heart failure at age forty-six.

Rex Stout's Stout Creation

Nero Wolfe is described in various places as weighing between 250 and 320 pounds.

However much he weighs, drinking five quarts of beer a day can't help.

Boozing Before Bar

Q: Which alcoholic divorcée wrote crime stories about cigar-smoking, booze-guzzling, womanizing Chicago lawyer John J. Malone under a male pseudonym—and in so doing opened the doors for generations of future female lethal thriller writers?

A: Georgiana Ann Randolph, who wrote the Malone series under the pseudonym Craig Rice, including such popular novels as:

- *8 Faces at Three* (1939)
- *Trial by Fury* (1941)
- *The Big Midget Murders* (1942)
- *The Fourth Postman* (1948)

The Sinful Life of a Writer

Craig Rice is definitely one of those crime writers who is as interesting and lively as her characters. Born in Chicago to an artist and socialite, Rice became alcohol dependent at an early age and reportedly went through seven husbands. Sadly, she died quite young in 1957 at the age of forty-nine.

Like Mother, Like Malone

Rice's lawyer-detective John J. Malone, however, lives on. Although he is an excellent attorney who would never leave a client hanging, Malone is as familiar with booze and women as Rice was with booze and husbands. Malone is a heavy drinker, making rye his pleasure. He likes the ladies and the ladies like him. He also has a collection of drinking "buddies," one of whom is a woman, Helene Brand; the other is Jake Justus.

> *"Alcohol is like love: the first kiss is magic, the second is intimate, the third is routine. After that, you just take the girl's clothes off."* —RAYMOND CHANDLER

Chicago: The Windy City of Sin

Rice's portrayal of Chicago is all her own. The Mafia is funny and the cops don't necessarily like to be Irish. Three movies were made about John J. Malone:

- *Having a Wonderful Crime* (1945)
- *The Lucky Stiff* (1949)
- *Mrs. O'Malley and Mr. Malone* (1950)

The stories even found their way to television in 1951–1952.

> *"Part of the $10 million I spent on gambling, part on booze, and part on women. The rest I spent foolishly."* —GEORGE RAFT

Bartender? I'll Have Another

The hard-drinking private investigator is so common that it has become a motif of the genre, which doesn't mean alcoholism hasn't been handled in various ways:

- What's one more hangover? In Dashiell Hammett's *The Thin Man* (1988), Nick and Nora Charles drink their way through the investigation with little ill effect.
- Damn this hangover! Jonathan Latimer's P.I. Bill Crane, on the other hand, feels the effects of the booze.
- No more hangovers. Finally, Lawrence Block's Matt Scudder is an alcoholic who decides to quit in *Eight Million Ways to Die* (2007).

The Quotable P.I.

General Sternwood: *How do you like your brandy, sir?*
Philip Marlowe: *In a glass.* —HUMPHREY BOGART AS P.I. PHILIP MARLOWE AND CHARLES WALDRON AS GENERAL STERNWOOD IN *THE BIG SLEEP* (1946)

COP TALK: DONUTS AND MORE

James "Jimmy" McNulty: *Can I get a Jameson?*
Bartender: *Bushmills okay?*
McNulty: *That's Protestant whiskey.*
—DOMINIC WEST AS DETECTIVE JAMES "JIMMY" MCNULTY IN *THE WIRE* (2002–2008)

Bad Bubbly

Q: In which episode of *Columbo* (1971–2003) does the rumpled detective solve a murder involving poisoned champagne?
A: "Publish or Perish" (1974), with guest star Jack Cassidy as the delightfully evil publisher out for revenge when his star writer jumps ship

The Quotable P.I.

"Morpheus' gifts used to come to me in bottles, Beam and black Jack Daniel's, straight up with a frosted schooner of Jax on the side, while I watched the rain pour down in the neon glow outside the window of an all-night bar not far from the Huey Long Bridge. In a half hour I could kick open a furnace door and fling into the flames all the snakes and squeaking bats that lived inside me. Except the next morning they would writhe with new life in the ashes and come back home, stinking and hungry." —DAVE ROBICHEAUX IN *A MORNING FOR FLAMINGOS* (1990) BY JAMES LEE BURKE

Extra Credit

Q: Which real-life author played the star writer in "Publish or Perish" (1974)?
A: Mickey Spillane, creator of the bestselling Mike Hammer novels

◌ *First Lines*

"I was off-duty at the time, sitting in a speak on South Clark Street drinking rum out of a coffee cup." —*TRUE DETECTIVE* (2003) BY MAX ALLAN COLLINS

COP TALK: DONUTS AND MORE

Helen Cruger: *Do you still drink coffee?*
Det. Frank Keller: *Like it's going out of style.*
—AL PACINO AS DETECTIVE FRANK KELLER AND ELLEN BARKIN AS HELEN CRUGER IN *SEA OF LOVE* (1989)

Corked!

Arachnophobes are more fearful of spiders than of death itself. But you are far more likely to die from a wayward champagne cork than from a poisonous spider bite.

◌ *First Lines*

"The first time I laid eyes on Terry Lennox he was drunk in a Rolls-Royce Silver Wraith outside the terrace of The Dancers." —*THE LONG GOODBYE* (1953) BY RAYMOND CHANDLER

DIY Murder Dinner Party

You can throw your own murder mystery party with *The Champagne Murders*, just one of the Inspector McClue Murder Mystery dinner party games.

The Sip of Death

Slipping poison into your intended victim's champagne is a classic means of murder. Here are five delicious mysteries in which sparkling wine delivers death's blow:

1. *Christmas Party* (1957) by Rex Stout
2. *Sparkling Cyanide* (1945) by Agatha Christie
3. *Now You See It . . .* (1995) by Richard Matheson
4. *Champagne for One* (1958) by Rex Stout
5. *Too Many Cooks* (1938) by Rex Stout

Harry Potter and the Duchess in the Poison Garden

The site where Harry Potter and all the young wizards brew their potions is—in real life—adjacent to a garden devoted to monkshood, foxglove, datura, mandrake root, and dozens of other plants that can cure or kill. Alnwick (pronounced AN-ihk) Castle is the ancestral home of the Dukes of Northumberland and the stand-in for the exteriors and interiors of Hogwarts. Next door is the Alnwick Garden with its world-famous Poison Garden, modeled after one built by the Medici in Padua, Italy.

Jane, the present Duchess of Northumberland, is an ardent horticulturist and the instigator of the Poison Garden, which opened to the public in 2004.

> *"My husband sometimes says he is worried about my knowledge of poison, but I tell him he shouldn't be concerned because these days every single plant poison is detectable in the blood."* —JANE, DUCHESS OF NORTHUMBERLAND

Forget Undead . . . I Want My Fiction Deadly

The Poison Diaries by Maryrose Wood is the first of a series of young adult novels set in the fictional gardens of Alnwick Castle in the 1700s. The idea for the books about a character who can communicate with the deadly plants came from the Duchess of Northumberland.

> *"I love the old way best, the simple way of poison, where we too are strong as men."* —EURIPIDES, *MEDEA*

No Thanks, I'm Stuffed

The present Duchess of Northumberland also has a taxidermy collection including twenty dogs, a squirrel, a rat, and a bird-eating spider.

Name Your Poison

Most folks know better than to taste-test anything labeled arsenic, cyanide, or strychnine, and they'd be leery of most plants with names like Toadroot, Witch's Gloves, Dead Tongue, or Devil's Ear. But see if you can match these English folk names to some of nature's prettiest plants and deadliest poisons:

1. Upright Virgin's Bower
2. Fairy Thimbles
3. Christmas Rose
4. Quaker Buttons
5. True Love
6. Naked Ladies
7. Memory Root

a. Meadow Saffron
b. Foxglove
c. American Wake-Robin
d. Paris Herb
e. Black Hellebore
f. Nux Vomica
g. Clematis

ANSWERS: 1-g; 2-b; 3-e; 4-f; 5-d; 6-a; 7-c

> *"The coward's weapon, poison."* —JOHN FLETCHER

Tasty Award-Winning P.I. Fiction
- *Sugartown* (2001) by Loren D. Estleman
- *Jersey Tomatoes* (1986) by J. W. Rider
- *Death on the Rocks* (1987) by Michael Allegretto
- *Served Cold* (1999) by Ed Goldberg
- *Big Red Tequila* (1996) by Rick Riordan

Wash Your Hands Before You Eat

Customers buying soap in Leonarda Cianciulli's small shop or visitors munching tea cakes in her home never suspected they were handling the remains of three women poisoned and chopped to pieces by the sweet, motherly Italian lady. The infamous "Soap-Maker of Correggio" was a rather sad and probably mad woman who came to believe that she could protect her oldest son from death in World War II by blood sacrifice.

From 1939 to 1940, she killed three neighbors who believed she had found them husbands or jobs in other towns. She mixed their blood with other ingredients to make tea cakes and rendered the flesh in a pot with caustic soda to make soap. She was tried for murder in 1946 and died in a criminal asylum for women in 1970.

> *"Her flesh was fat and white, when it had melted I added a bottle of cologne, and after a long time on the boil I was able to make some most acceptable creamy soap. I gave bars to neighbours and acquaintances. The cakes, too, were better: that woman was really sweet."* —LEONARDA CIANCIULLI

DEADLY DIALOGUE

Richard Castle: *You have to admit, putting a body in an oven is a clever way to get rid of it.* —NATHAN FILLION AS RICHARD CASTLE IN *CASTLE* (2009–)

COP TALK: DONUTS AND MORE

Holly McClane: *Honey, it's the nineties, remember? Microchips, microwaves, faxes, *air phones*.*

John McClane: *Hey, well, as far as I'm concerned, progress peaked with frozen pizza.*

—BRUCE WILLIS AS LIEUTENANT JOHN MCCLANE AND BONNIE BEDELIA AS HOLLY MCCLANE IN *DIE HARD 2* (1990)

Beware Mom's Home Cooking

"Trust none of the dishes at dinner: Those pies are steaming-black with the poison Mummy put there. Whatever she offers you, make sure another person tries it out first. . . . What I can't stand is the calculating woman who plans her crimes in cold blood." —*THE SIXTEEN SATIRES* (C. 100 A.D.) BY JUVENAL

KILLER WIT

"Some of our most exquisite murders have been domestic, performed with tenderness in simple, homey places like the kitchen table."
—ALFRED HITCHCOCK

Starring a Great Leg of Lamb

One of the most unusual murder weapons in fiction is the leg of lamb used by Mary Maloney to dispatch her husband in Roald Dahl's short story, "Lamb to the Slaughter," later presented as an episode on television's *Alfred Hitchcock Presents*.

◊ First Lines

"The room was warm and clean, the curtains drawn, the two table lamps alight —hers and the one by the empty chair opposite. On the sideboard behind her, two tall glasses, soda water, whiskey. Fresh ice cubes in the Thermos bucket.

"Mary Maloney was waiting for her husband to come home from work."
—"LAMB TO THE SLAUGHTER" (1953) BY ROALD DAHL

Note to Cop: Don't Eat the Murder Weapon!

After blonking her philandering policeman-husband in the back of the head with the frozen leg of lamb, Roald Dahl's fictional creation Mary Maloney put it in her oven. Then she went to the grocer's, told him she was fixing a meal for her husband, and bought some vegetables and a slice of cheesecake. Returning home, she called the police about the murder of her husband by an intruder while she was at the store. When his fellow policemen arrived, they carefully checked her alibi with the grocer and went in search of the murder weapon. As one of them told her, "Get the weapon, and you've got the man." Well, they couldn't find the weapon and, after a long search, they were tired and hungry. Mary insisted they eat the lamb, now fully cooked. She said her husband would have wanted them to. So they did, talking about how the murder weapon must have been so big that it should be easy to find. One added that it might be right under their noses. Mary, listening in the other room, giggled.

Are You Feeling Lucky?

Then name the Dirty Harry movie from which the following dialogue is drawn:

Harry Callahan: You know what makes me really sick to my stomach?
Burly Detective: What?
Harry: Is watching you stuff your face with those hot dogs. Nobody, I mean *nobody*, puts ketchup on a hot dog.

ANSWER: *Sudden Impact* (1983)

Feast Yourself on These Police Procedurals

- *The Artful Egg* (1984) by James H. McClure
- *Behold, Here's Poison* (1936) by Georgette Heyer
- *The Bottom of the Bottle* (1977) by Georges Simenon
- *Death of a Glutton* (1993) by M. C. Beaton
- *Fruits of the Poisonous Tree* (1993) by Archer Mayor
- *Madam Will Not Dine Tonight* (1947) by Hillary Waugh
- *The Second Deadly Sin* (1977) by Lawrence Sanders
- *The Snack Thief* (1996) by Andrea Camilleri
- *Sugar & Spice* (2003) by Keith Lee Johnson
- *A Taste for Death* (1986) by P. D. James

COP TALK: DONUTS AND MORE

Hap Eckhart: *We got the Halibut Calabrese, the Halibut Olympian.*
Will Dormer: *Keep going.*
Eckhart: *Halibut Cajun style.*
Dormer: *I can't wait to see what they got for dessert.* —AL PACINO AS LAPD DETECTIVE WILL DORMER AND MARTIN DONOVAN AS DETECTIVE HAP ECKHART IN *INSOMNIA* (2002)

Doctor, Lawyer, Glutton

Could anything seem more professionally gluttonous than being a lawyer and a doctor all at the same time? R. Austin Freeman's character Dr. John Thorndyke, like his creator, is both lawyer and doctor. Freeman was such a stickler for details he would actually have murder contraptions built and tested—short of killing someone—before using them in his stories.

"Gluttony is a great fault; but we do not necessarily dislike a glutton. We only dislike the glutton when he becomes a gourmet—that is, we only dislike him when he not only wants the best for himself, but knows what is best for other people." —G. K. CHESTERTON

Cat and Mouse Games

Q: Which sub-genre of mystery is Freeman credited with creating?
A: The inverted mystery, in which readers know who the killer is and the suspense lies in the cat-and-mouse capture of the killer.

Chandler on Freeman

"Austin Freeman is a wonderful performer. He has no equal in his genre." —RAYMOND CHANDLER, HIGH PRAISE FOR THE VOCAL CRITIC OF THE TRADITIONAL DETECTIVE STORY

Move Over, Sherlock Holmes

Although never as popular as the Holmes canon, fan groups and readers all over the world keep the good lawyer/doctor in fine fettle, making him a true cornerstone character in medical-jurist literature. While all the Thorndyke canon stands up as a whole, some of the more notable Thorndyke stories include:

- *The Red Thumb Mark* (1907)
- *The Eye of Osiris* (1911)
- *The Cat's Eye* (1923)
- *Mr. Pottermack's Oversight* (1930)
- *The Jacob Street Mystery* (1942)

Call Me Anything You Want, But Don't Call Me Late for Dinner

- Private Investigator
- P.I.
- Private Eye
- Private Dick
- Detective
- Operative
- Shamus
- Sherlock
- Gumshoe
- Bottomfeeder

Murder on the Menu

"Fourteen delicious private eye tales guaranteed to whet your appetite for detection.

"Wining, dining, and death. Fast living and fine dining combine to present today's private eyes with culinary crimes suitable for even the most refined palate. The private eyes in these stories face delicious dangers, savory sins, and tasty temptations . . . and the bad guys always get their just desserts. An appetizing selection of today's top private eye writers and talented newcomers season their tales with the exciting spices of love, hate, justice, and vengeance. Here are fourteen delicious private eye tales— and one poem—guaranteed to whet your appetite for detection." —FROM *HARDBROILED* (2003), AN ANTHOLOGY OF PRIVATE EYE STORIES THAT CENTER AROUND FOOD

The Quotable P.I.

"I stir up trouble on the side." —DICK POWELL AS P.I. PHILIP MARLOWE IN *MURDER, MY SWEET* (1944)

The Quotable P.I.

"Except for cases that clearly involve a homicidal maniac, the police like to believe murders are committed by those we know and love, and most of the time they're right—a chilling thought when you sit down to dinner with a family of five. All those potential killers passing their plates." —INSEY MILLHONE IN *A IS FOR ALIBI* (1982) BY SUE GRAFTON

BLOOD & BONES

"I love to enter the crime scene from the kitchen. People's minute-to-minute movements are registered here. I routinely open the refrigerator to get people's lifestyles: the type of food they like, where they buy, how much they pay, how they wrap. In one homicide I investigated, the homeowner returned early, surprising the burglar, so the burglary ended in murder. But the burglar was hungry, so he had a bite to eat before leaving. We found distinct teeth marks in the cheese!" —DR. THOMAS NOGUCHI

DEADLY DIALOGUE

Scott Turner: *Don't eat the car! Not the car! Oh, what am I yelling at you for? You're a dog!* —TOM HANKS AS DETECTIVE SCOTT TURNER IN *TURNER & HOOCH* (1989)

KILLER WIT

"The length of a film should be directly related to the endurance of the human bladder."

—ALFRED HITCHCOCK

⍥ *First Lines*

"Context is everything. Dress me up and see. I'm a carnival barker, an auctioneer, a downtown performance artist, a speaker in tongues, a senator drunk on filibuster." —*MOTHERLESS BROOKLYN* (1999) BY JONATHAN LETHEM

Are You Feeling Lucky?

Then name the Dirty Harry movie from which the following dialogue is drawn:

Waiter: This poor man's had a heart attack. I think he's still breathing, though.

Harry Callahan: *[Starts kicking Customer #1 in the ribs]* Come on, get up. Get up! Get up. Come on.

Waiter: What are you doing?

Harry: Come on, get up, get up, get up! Come on! *[Yanks Customer #1 to his feet.]*

Customer #2: I say!

Harry: *[Pulling Customer #1 out of the restaurant]* Party's over.

Freddie the Fainter: Thanks a lot, Harry.

Harry: What are you squawking about? You got the free meal, didn't you?

Freddie the Fainter: Yeah, but I always enjoy that ride in the ambulance.

Harry: Get out of here.

ANSWER: *Dirty Harry* (1971)

COP TALK: DONUTS AND MORE

Martin Riggs: *Well, what do you wanna hear, man? Do you wanna hear that sometimes I think about eatin' a bullet? Huh? Well, I do!* —MEL GIBSON AS SERGEANT MARTIN RIGGS IN *LETHAL WEAPON* (1987)

❧ *First Lines*

"*The fire began at sunset.*

"*It filled the house like a hot putrid breath, alive. It ran like a liquid through the place, stopping at nothing, feeding on everything in its path, irreverent and unforgiving. It raced like a phantom, room to room, eating the drapes, the rugs, the towels, the sheet, and linens, the clothes, the shoes, and blankets in the closets, removing any and all evidence of things human.*" —*BEYOND RECOGNITION* (1997) BY RIDLEY PEARSON

"Murder is always a mistake—one should never do anything one cannot talk about after dinner." —OSCAR WILDE

GREED

n., from the Old English *gradig,* meaning voracious

1. Excessive desire to accumulate more of something than one deserves, especially material goods
2. Insatiable desire for wealth; avarice

"Tell me, is there some society you know of that doesn't run on greed?"
—MILTON FRIEDMAN

Greed is good . . . for the bad guys. In fact, greed is the driving force behind many a crime—and virtually all of our so-called white-collar crime. Money may not be the root of all evil, but it is certainly the root of all greed—as more than one victim in possession of a good fortune has found out the hard way.

KILLER WIT

"When an actor comes to me and wants to discuss his character, I say, 'It's in the script.' If he says, 'But what's my motivation?' I say, 'Your salary.'"
—ALFRED HITCHCOCK

A Thousand a Day, Plus Expenses

"Median annual wages of salaried private detectives and investigators were $41,760 in May 2008. The middle 50 percent earned between $30,870 and $59,060. The lowest 10 percent earned less than $23,500, and the highest 10 percent earned more than $76,640. Wages of private detectives and investigators vary greatly by employer, specialty, and geographic area." (Source: *Occupational Outlook Handbook, 2010–11 Edition*, Bureau of Labor Statistics)

◌ *First Lines*

"It is a truth universally acknowledged that a private investigator who acts on his own behalf is an idiot who has a fool for a client." —THE MEMORY BOOK (2006) BY HOWARD ENGEL

◌ *First Lines*

"Ray Cuervo sat in his office and counted his money. He counted his money every Friday afternoon between five and six o'clock. He made no secret of it." —SHADOW PREY (1990) BY JOHN SANFORD

You Get How Much?

In fiction, private investigators don't necessarily fare much better.

- Encyclopedia Brown, Donald J. Sobol's kid-genius detective, charged $0.25 per case.
- Philip Marlowe started charging $25 a day plus expenses but raised his rates during World War II to $50 a day plus expenses.
- Jim Rockford charged $200 a day plus expenses.
- And Nero Wolfe? "I do not soil myself cheaply; I charge high fees." (*Too Many Cooks* [1938] by Rex Stout)

The Quotable P.I. _____

Marlowe: *I could make it my business.*

Mars: *I could make your business mine.*

Marlowe: *But you wouldn't like it. The pay's too small.* —HUMPHREY BOGART AS P.I. PHILIP MARLOWE IN *THE BIG SLEEP* (1946)

When Is Enough Enough?

If ever there was a case of Greed on the one hand being punished by Excess on the other, it is recorded in the atrocities committed by Jehu (2 Kings 9–10). The chain of events was set in motion by King Ahab, who coveted a neighboring vineyard but could not persuade its owner, Naboth, to trade or sell it. Ahab's delightful wife, the infamous Queen Jezebel, contrived Naboth's execution on false charges and then sent her husband to claim the dead man's property. There he was confronted by the prophet Elijah, who cursed Ahab.

> *"This is what the Lord says: In the place where dogs licked up Naboth's blood, dogs will lick up your blood—yes, yours!"* —1 KINGS 21:19 NIV

Sure Enough . . .

Three years later, when Ahab tried to grab more property, this time the city of Ramoth-Gilead, he was struck by an arrow and died in his chariot. The chariot was washed out on the spot where Naboth died. Yes, there were dogs.

Seventy Beheaded Heads of State

Turned out "your blood" also meant "your descendants." Enter Jehu, anointed by order of the prophet Elisha and given the job of wiping out all of Ahab and Jezebel's blood. He killed their son, King Joram (already wounded in another attempt to take Ramoch-Gilead), and had his body tossed into Naboth's vineyard. He persuaded the palace eunuchs to throw Jezebel into the courtyard and trampled her body under horse and chariot, leaving the rest for the dogs. Next he ordered the beheading of seventy princes of the blood and eventually slew assorted relatives, supporters, and hangers-on. He ruled for twenty-eight years.

Not Named for a Murderer

Jehu is not a popular name for babies. Anywhere.

> *"Murderers, in general, are people who are consistent, people who are obsessed with one idea and nothing else."* —UGO BETTI

> *"It is greed to do all the talking but not to want to listen at all."*
> —DEMOCRITUS

Stranger Than Fiction

Q: What historic murder case was given an alternate interpretation in the award-winning Anita Shreve novel and subsequent movie, *The Weight of Water* (2000)?

A: On a cold March night in 1873, two Norwegian women were killed on Smuttynose Island off the coast of New Hampshire. Maren Hontvedt survived the attack that killed her sister and sister-in-law, Karen and Anethe Christensen. She said that Louis Wagner, a fisherman who had worked for and lived with the Hontvedts, had broken into her home on a night he knew the men were in Portsmouth waiting for a bait shipment. He believed the Hontvedts had money hidden away and killed the women to cover up his theft. Wagner fled to Boston, but he was arrested, tried, and executed for the murders. In Shreve's novel, a photojournalist, researching the case as a tie-in to a modern double murder, discovers Maren's secret written account of what happened that night. As her own life parallels the events she is reading about, will Smuttynose witness another tragedy?

First Lines

"It is my job to see if I see a shape, a rocky ledge, an island." —THE *WEIGHT OF WATER* (1997) BY ANITA SHREVE

> *"The night before the murder he was penniless and unkempt. The day following the murder Wagner shaved his beard, hopped a train to Boston and was apprehended wearing brand new clothes."* —DENNIS J. ROBINSON, "WHY LOUIS WAGNER WAS SMUTTYNOSE SLAYER" (2008) ON SEACOASTNH.COM

Homicide

n.: The slaying of one human being by another. There are four kinds of homicide: felonious, excusable, justifiable, and praiseworthy, but it makes no great difference to the person slain whether he fell by one kind or another—the classification is for advantage of the lawyers.
—**AMBROSE BIERCE,** *DEVIL'S DICTIONARY* (1911)

"Murder is not the crime of criminals, but that of law-abiding citizens."
—EMMANUEL TENEY

Neither a Borrower Nor a Greedy Lender Bleed

Q: In which Shakespeare play does one of the first great lawyers of literature—a woman, not a man—appear?

A: In a world dominated by male lawyers—both the real world and the one found only in fantasy—Shakespeare's *The Merchant of Venice* is an anomaly. In this groundbreaking play, a debtor cannot repay his loan to a greedy creditor. Per the loan agreement the debtor must give the creditor a pound of his flesh. To remedy the dispute, the Duke of Venice, who takes an interest in the case, sends for a legal expert, whom he believes is a man. The legal expert, however, is really the debtor's sweetheart, Portia, disguised as a man. Portia reasons with the greedy creditor that while he is entitled to the pound of flesh he has not contracted to shed any of the debtor's blood, proving that Hell hath no fury like the wrath of a female lawyer. Eat your heart out, Jack McCoy and Mickey Haller, and spill all the blood you want—you guys got nothin' on Portia!

Legalese at Its Best

> *"Take thou thy pound of flesh; But, in the cutting it, if thou dost shed One drop of Christian blood, thy lands and goods Are, by the law of Venice, confiscate Unto the state of Venice."* —PORTIA IN *THE MERCHANT OF VENICE*, ACT IV, SCENE I, BY WILLIAM SHAKESPEARE

> *"Where large sums of money are concerned, it is advisable to trust nobody."* —AGATHA CHRISTIE

Greed Takes the Stand

Is being lonely really all that dangerous? It is if you fall under the spell of a sinister, greedy ne'er-do-well. Hence the plot for Dame Agatha Christie's remarkable courtroom 1948 short story, "The Witness for the Prosecution."

Greed in a Nutshell

In "The Witness for the Prosecution," famous British barrister Sir Wilfrid Robarts is recovering from a heart attack. He is under strict doctor's orders to stay away from any stressful trial. But he can't. It's his life. So when the suave Leonard Vole is arrested for the murder of a wealthy, middle-aged widow—her money being the motive—Sir Wilfrid can't resist the challenge.

The evidence is stacked against his client, but Sir Wilfrid masterfully gnaws away at the facts during one of the most dramatic and unusual trials ever penned.

Ask Yourself . . .

- Is Sir Wilfrid's client the greedy reprobate the prosecution has portrayed him as?
- Is the fact that his own wife testifies against him going to deny him an acquittal and sully the reputation of one of England's most respected and proudest barristers?
- Will greed ultimately win the day?

All signs point to "yes," but Sir Wilfrid is not without a few trial tricks of his own.

Greed on the Screen

Q: Who starred in the 1957 film version of *Witness for the Prosecution*?
A: Tyrone Power as the hard-luck Leonard Vole, Marlene Dietrich as Vole's scorned wife, and the larger-than-life Charles Laughton as Sir Wilfrid Robarts. The story was also adapted for a TV movie in 1982 starring Ralph Richardson as Sir Wilfrid.

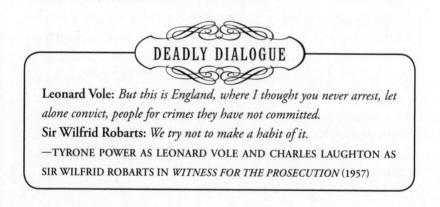

DEADLY DIALOGUE

Leonard Vole: *But this is England, where I thought you never arrest, let alone convict, people for crimes they have not committed.*
Sir Wilfrid Robarts: *We try not to make a habit of it.*
—TYRONE POWER AS LEONARD VOLE AND CHARLES LAUGHTON AS SIR WILFRID ROBARTS IN *WITNESS FOR THE PROSECUTION* (1957)

> *"The small man wore white from the tip of his pointed hat to the rolled-up cuffs of his baggy trousers."* —HEART OF THE WORLD (2006) BY LINDA BARNES

Holler for Haller

Q: If you're a scumbag in fictional Los Angeles, who do you call when you get caught?

A: Mickey Haller, lawyer to drug dealers, flim flammers, drunk drivers, and that most sympathetic defendant of all—the murderer. L.A. defense attorney Mickey Haller is the creation of Edgar winner and past president of the Mystery Writers of America Michael Connelly. For Haller, the law is (as Connelly explains it), "[R]arely about guilt or innocence—it's about negotiation and manipulation." The strength of Connelly's Haller novels lies in their superior characterization, plotting, suspense, and dead-on authenticity concerning the inner workings of the criminal justice system.

> *"What is overriding that and most important is that readers generally are interested in a good character. They might be more comfortable with Harry [Hieronymus Bosch] because they think they know him, but they always seem willing to give somebody new a chance."* —MICHAEL CONNELLY, ON MICHAEL HALLER

The Quotable P.I.

Mike Hammer: *What's in it for me?* —RALPH MEEKER AS P.I. MIKE HAMMER IN *KISS ME DEADLY* (1955)

Name your favorite Haller book:

- *The Lincoln Lawyer* (2005)
- *The Brass Verdict* (2008)
- *The Reversal* (2010)
- *The Fifth Witness* (2011)

Matthew McConaughey—Type Casting?

The Lincoln Lawyer has been adapted for the big screen starring bad boy himself Matthew McConaughey.

Edgar Loves Connelly

Q: For which novel did Michael Connelly win the coveted Edgar Allan Poe Award for Best First Novel in 1992?

A: *The Black Echo* (1992), the debut of the popular series starring LAPD Detective Hieronymus "Harry" Bosch

---

COP TALK: GREED IS GOOD

Nick Conklin: *A couple of guys I used to work with in the department took some money from some drug dealers. No big deal.*

Matsumoto Masahiro: *They stole?*

Nick: *They liberated funds.*

Masahiro: *Theft is theft. There is no gray area.*

Nick: *Hey Matsu, New York is one big gray area.*

—MICHAEL DOUGLAS AS OFFICER NICK CONKLIN AND KEN TAKAKURA

AS OFFICER MATSUMOTO MASAHIRO IN *BLACK RAIN* (1989)

When Good Guys Go Bad

Name the films in which the following law enforcement officers go lawless:

1. Gary Oldman plays Stansfield, a crooked cop who wipes out an entire family with the exception of a young girl who escapes into the arms of a professional hit man.
2. David Soul plays Officer John Davis, Robert Urich plays Officer Mike Grimes, and Tim Matheson plays Officer Phil Sweet, three traffic cops who take the law in their own hands. Only "Dirty" Harry Callahan has what it takes to bring them down.
3. Harvey Keitel plays Lieutenant Ray Donlan, a crooked cop from New York City who's created a safe haven for other dirty cops in nearby New Jersey. Since NYPD Internal Affairs officer Lieutenant Moe Tilden (played by Robert De Niro) has no jurisdiction across the river, he's forced to use Sheriff Freddy Heflin (Sylvester Stallone playing against type) to bring Donlan to justice.
4. Richard Gere plays corrupt LAPD Officer Dennis Peck, his extravagant lifestyle making him an easy target for Andy Garcia playing Internal Affairs detective Raymond Avilla.
5. Denzel Washington plays Detective Sergeant Alonzo Harris, a veteran cop who shows rookie Jake Hoyt (Ethan Hawke) the wrong ropes.
6. Harvey Keitel plays a homicide detective on the skids who needs one last chance to redeem himself.
7. Orson Welles plays corrupt police chief Hank Quinlan who tangles with Charlton Heston playing narcotics officer Mike Vargas.
8. Matt Damon plays a crooked cop infiltrating Massachusetts State Police at the behest of mobster Frank Costello (Jack Nicholson). One of his duties is to find the cop who's infiltrated Costello's mob.
9. Al Pacino plays NYPD officer Frank Serpico, a good cop who becomes determined to root out the corruption on the force.
10. While LA detective Jack Vincennes (Kevin Spacey) may accept bribes, his crimes pale when compared to those committed by James Cromwell playing Dudley Smith.

ANSWERS: 1) *Leon: The Professional* (1994); 2) *Magnum Force* (1973); 3) *Cop Land* (1997); 4) *Internal Affairs* (1990); 5) *Training Day* (2001); 6) *Bad Lieutenant* (1992); 7) *Touch of Evil* (1958); 8) *The Departed* (2006); 9) *Serpico* (1973); 10) *L.A. Confidential* (1997)

COP TALK: MACHISMO SPEAKS!

James "Jimmy" McNulty: *You know what they call a guy who pays that much attention to his clothes, don't you?*

William "Bunk" Moreland: *A grown-up.*

—DOMINIC WEST AS DETECTIVE JAMES "JIMMY" MCNULTY AND WENDELL PIERCE AS DETECTIVE BUNK MORELAND IN *THE WIRE* (2002–2008)

The Quotable P.I.

Sam Spade: *We didn't exactly believe your story, Miss O'Shaughnessy; we believed your two hundred dollars . . . I mean, you paid us more than if you'd been telling us the truth, and enough more to make it all right.*

—HUMPHREY BOGART AS P.I. SAM SPADE IN *THE MALTESE FALCON* (1941)

Coked-Up Evidence

If you had to get caught dealing drugs, San Francisco was the place to be in 2010, especially if the evidence against you went to criminalist Deborah Madden. That's when Madden was accused of pilfering small amounts of cocaine from the lab for personal use. An internal review turned up significant shortages of drug evidence in several cases she handled. But Madden said she was not surprised by that because weight discrepancies occurred frequently at the lab. The San Francisco district attorney's office first said a half-dozen cases might be compromised, then began to drop hundreds of cases. Later, the investigation of the lab expanded to look at the potential involvement of other crime lab employees, and the DA's office had to analyze 1,400 pending felony narcotics cases they might be forced to drop. Madden retired and no charges were filed.

Move Over, Dirty Harry

In March of 2011, San Francisco prosecutors said they were dropping dozens more cases handled by a group of police officers who are accused of conducting illegal searches on suspects, and investigators were looking into whether more could be implicated in the scandal.

An afternoon court hearing was scheduled to formally dismiss the felony and misdemeanor cases, which would bring the total to fifty-seven dropped.

Seven officers and a sergeant were under federal and local investigation for raiding rooms without warrants at a downtown residential hotel notorious for drug activity. Hotel surveillance video of some of the raids surfaced last week.

District Attorney George Gascón, who was police chief when the alleged incidents occurred, said charges in the felony cases could be refiled, though his office likely would no longer pursue the dropped misdemeanors. Most were drug cases, though some were robberies and assaults, Gascón noted. None was a homicide.

> *"These alleged acts of misconduct committed by these officers have great ramifications."* —SAN FRANCISCO PUBLIC DEFENDER JEFF ADACHI IN A LETTER TO DISTRICT ATTORNEY GEORGE GASCÓN

If You Must Have More Police Procedurals:

- *Blood Money* (1999) by Rochelle Majer Krich
- *Bread* (1974) by Ed McBain
- *City for Ransom* (2006) by Robert W. Walker
- *Final Payment* (2007) by Steven F. Havill
- *Five Pieces of Jade* (1972) by John Ball
- "If You've Got the Money, Honey, I've Got the Crime" (1994) by Barbara D'Amato

- *King's Ransom* (1959) by Ed McBain
- *Money, Money, Money* (2001) by Ed McBain
- *Payment in Blood* (1989) by Elizabeth George
- *The Price of Malice* (2009) by Archer Mayor
- *The Third Deadly Sin* (1981) by Lawrence Sanders

COP TALK: GREED IS GOOD

Leo Getz: *Okay, okay, okay, okay, this is the best part, okay? You make a tax deduction on interest payments you don't even make! Am I an innovator? Am I a genius?*

Martin Riggs: *You're a swindler!*

Roger Murtaugh: *Cheat!*

Getz: *Everyone cheats a little bit . . . look at the Pentagon!*

—MEL GIBSON AS SERGEANT MARTIN RIGGS, DANNY GLOVER AS SERGEANT ROGER MURTAUGH, AND JOE PESCI AS LEO GETZ IN *LETHAL WEAPON 2* (1989)

"Under the rules of a society that cannot distinguish between profit and profiteering, between money defined as necessity and money defined as luxury, murder is occasionally obligatory and always permissible."
—LEWIS H. LAPHAM, *MONEY AND CLASS IN AMERICA*

Dr. Jim and Rev. Sam: The Marrying Murderers

"Dr. Jim" Giesick was a particularly slimy wife-killer, a Texas conman who conspired with "Rev. Sam" Corey, an ersatz preacher, to marry, insure, and murder for the payoff any vulnerable young woman who fell into their trap.

After a blitzkrieg courtship, Giesick married naïve young Patricia Albanowski in January 1974 and hustled her off to New Orleans on their honeymoon. He took his bride for an evening stroll and pushed her into the path of a car driven by Corey.

Prompted by Patricia's suspicious parents, police detective John Dillman was eventually able to tie Giesick to a rental car with strands of Patricia's hair stuck to the undercarriage. Giesick made a deal for a lighter sentence and rolled on Corey, who got life.

Murdered for the Insurance

Match the victim to the book in which he/she/it gets murdered.

1. *Unholy Matrimony* (1986) by John Dillmann
2. *Double Indemnity* (1943) by James M. Cain
3. *Rock Roadie* (2009) by James "Tappy" Wright
4. *Story of My Life* (1988) by Jay McInerney
5. *Blind Faith* (1989) by Joe McGinniss

a. Mr. Nirdlinger
b. Dangerous Dan
c. Jimi Hendrix
d. Maria Marshall
e. Patricia Albanowski

ANSWERS 1-e; 2-a; 3-c; 4-b; 5-d

How Poisonous Is a Black Widow?

Women who systematically murder family members or intimates are known as "Black Widows" and they are truly deadly.

- Average number of victims: 6–8 in the United States and ranging into the hundreds
- Average age at first kill: 35–40
- Active "killing" phase: 10-plus years

- Victims of choice: spouse(s), lover(s), children, parents, elderly dependents
- Method of choice: poison
- Motives: profit, convenience, jealousy, attention

The Quotable P.I.

John "Scottie" Ferguson: *You shouldn't keep souvenirs of a killing. You shouldn't have been that sentimental.* " —JAMES STEWART AS P.I. JOHN "SCOTTIE" FERGUSON IN *VERTIGO* (1958)

Death Benefits

She was never arrested or charged with a single crime, but Belle Gunness is recognized as one of the deadliest serial killers in criminal history. Born in Norway in 1859 to a family always teetering on the brink of ruin, she immigrated to the United States at age twenty-one, married, and seemed to be content. In 1896, her husband's new confectionary business was failing when two disasters struck the family: their oldest child died suddenly and mysteriously, and the sweet shop was destroyed in a fire. Both were insured.

Two years later, the family's new home burned to the ground and another child died mysteriously. In 1890, Belle's husband died. She collected benefits on all three occasions. Belle moved her children to an Indiana farm, where she continued her murders for money. Her second husband met with a fatal accident, and many of the farm workers who answered Belle's advertisements were never seen again.

In 1908 the Gunness farmhouse was destroyed by fire. The bodies of Belle's three children and the decapitated corpse of a woman were found in the basement. Within a month, investigators had started digging up the remains of at least sixteen people and possibly twelve more. Most of the females had been buried, but some of the males had been fed to the hogs.

The Ballad of Belle Gunness

> *"But hogs were just a sideline*
> *She indulged in now and then;*
> *Her favorite occupation*
> *Was a-butchering of men."*
>
> —UNKNOWN, "BELLE GUNNESS"

They Called Her Lady Bluebeard

Belle Gunness, "Lady Bluebeard," may have murdered as many as forty-nine people, including her husbands and children. The headless corpse was never positively identified as hers.

A Macabre Footnote

When Gunness's close friend and neighbor died in 1916, a woman's skull was found in her home, wedged between two mattresses.

The Quotable P.I. ─────────────

John Shaft: *I thought the money didn't matter to you. Just getting your baby back.*

Bumpy Jonas: *Money ALWAYS matters . . .*

—RICHARD ROUNDTREE AS P.I. JOHN SHAFT AND MOSES GUNN AS BUMPY JONAS IN *SHAFT* (1971)

Did King Richard III Kill the Princes in the Tower— or Not?

They say history is written by the victors; in the case of Richard III, that's true only if you take the long view. Richard III has always been accused by the Tudors—who succeeded him—of killing his young nephews Edward V of England, Richard of Shrewsbury, 1st Duke of York, in order to secure his right to the throne. But the evidence is scanty—there were no bodies found, and more than one pretender came along after their supposed deaths. Not to mention that there were plenty of suspects to go around.

Historical Fiction Not Intended for Children

Several mystery writers have re-imagined the plight of the princes, in such works as:

- *The Daughter of Time* (1951) by Josephine Tey
- *I, Richard* (2001) by Elizabeth George
- *Sent* (2009) by Margaret Haddix
- *Crown of Roses* (1989) by Valerie Anand
- *The Murders of Richard III* (1989) by Elizabeth Peters
- *The Sunne in Splendour* (2007) by Sharon Kay Penman

⊗ *First Lines*

"Brother Cadfael set out from the gatehouse, that Monday afternoon of October, in the year 1139, darkly convinced that something ominous would have happened before he re-entered that great court, though he had no reason to suppose that he would be absent more than an hour or so." —THE LEPER OF SAINT GILES (1981) BY ELLIS PETERS

> *"All religion, my friend, is simply evolved out of fraud, fear, greed, imagination, and poetry."* —EDGAR ALLAN POE

The Case of the Greedy Writer

Q: What was one of Erle Stanley Gardner's greedy little secrets for marketing murder in the literary mainstream?

A: The lawyer, author, and creator of the *Perry Mason* series would hoard his ideas from would-be literary pirates. According to Gardner, he would keep closets chock-full of first-hand interviews with murderers, wardens, cops, and private eyes and then jealously guard the coveted material from other writers. After all, they might, Gardner said, "be able to do what I'm doing with this material." Considering that Gardner needed five secretaries in order to produce his works, clearly he never learned to share!

> *"It's a damn good story. If you have any comments, write them on the back of a check."* —ERLE STANLEY GARDNER

◎ *First Lines*

> *"The night sky was sodden with low-hanging clouds. Cold drizzle coated the sidewalks with moisture, gave a halo to the street lights, and caused the tires of passing automobiles to hiss over wet pavement."* —*THE CASE OF THE ONE-EYED WITNESS* (1950) BY ERLE STANLEY GARDNER

Put All the Greedy Solicitors in a Lockbox

What could possibly be more confining than a locked-room mystery? How about a lockbox mystery? English solicitor Michael Gilbert (who once served as Raymond Chandler's lawyer) had a prolific writing career spanning more than half a century. In one of his most famous novels,

Smallbone Deceased (1950), Gilbert spun a masterful "lockbox" mystery—a clever twist on the seemingly impossible circumstances of its locked-room cousins.

What's a Lockbox Mystery?

Gilbert must have been the envy of every mystery writer's eye when he managed to make suspects out of six lawyers in the tightly plotted *Smallbone Deceased*. The novel is centered around the cozy and discreet London solictors' office of Horniman, Birley and Crane—the type Gilbert practiced in for more than three decades. Cozy that is until one of the trustees, Marcus Smallbone, is found murdered and stuffed in a deed box. Tagged as an obvious inside job, scandal ensues when the members of the firm become the principal suspects.

Corporate Greed

Q: Which Boston-based legal thriller best captures the struggles lawyers have fighting corporate greed?

A: Boston attorney-writer Barry C. Reed's legal drama *The Verdict* (1980). Boston attorney Frank Galvin is an alcoholic, washout ambulance chaser who loses one case after another. Finally he picks up an easy medical malpractice suit against a major Boston hospital—a case where the hospital is willing to throw some money at it in order to make it go away. Some quick cash and Galvin's legal career is back on track. Then he studies the case and visits his client. A young woman will remain in a coma for the rest of her life because of a doctor's gross negligence. Galvin decides to resurrect his career as an attorney. He could grab the quick cash, but decides to do the right thing and expose the cover-up. He realizes that he is the only voice left for his client. Then all hell breaks loose.

Old Money Talks

Galvin's one-man firm must take on a prestigious Yankee law firm that will use any amount of money and tricks to bring Galvin down. A key witness disappears. One witness is too scared to testify. Documents are lost or forged. A cynical judge hell-bent on destroying Galvin throws up one roadblock after another in order to destroy his case. While *The Verdict* has memorable and powerful courtroom scenes, it also offers the shocking realities lawyers must confront before they get into a courtroom. In this case, certainly, corporate greed and pride do their best to dismantle Galvin.

From the Turn of a Page to the Edge of Your Seat

Q: Who starred in the movie version of *The Verdict?*
A: *The Verdict* was made into a movie in 1982 starring Paul Newman, Jack Warden, and James Mason and received numerous, well-deserved Oscar nominations for Best Actor, Best Supporting Actor, Best Director, Best Screenplay, and Best Picture.

"Lust and greed are more gullible than innocence." —MASON COOLEY

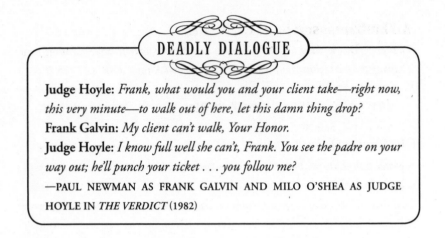

DEADLY DIALOGUE

Judge Hoyle: *Frank, what would you and your client take—right now, this very minute—to walk out of here, let this damn thing drop?*
Frank Galvin: *My client can't walk, Your Honor.*
Judge Hoyle: *I know full well she can't, Frank. You see the padre on your way out; he'll punch your ticket . . . you follow me?*
—PAUL NEWMAN AS FRANK GALVIN AND MILO O'SHEA AS JUDGE HOYLE IN *THE VERDICT* (1982)

If You're Greedy, Grab Two for the Price of One

If there is any lawyer who could both prosecute and defend a criminal brought before the bar, all at the same time, it has to be multi-Shamus award–winning author-lawyer Jeremiah Healy, a.k.a. Terry Devane. Healy immediately captured readers' attention in 1985 with the release of his first novel *Blunt Darts*, featuring Boston P.I. John Francis Cuddy.

Jerry or Terry?

As for legal thrillers, take your choice under Healy or his nom de plume Terry Devane. Healy's stand-alone *The Stalking of Sheila Quinn* (1998) is a shocking look at what it's like to be a female attorney stalked by the very defendant you got off the hook. His Cuddy P.I. series is as good a trip through the Boston P.I. world as anything from Parker's Spenser.

Under Devane, there's the Mairead O'Clare legal thriller series hailed as "sly and brilliant" by Jeffery Deaver. *Uncommon Justice* (2001) introduces O'Clare, who leaves big firm life to team up with an older criminal defense attorney, Sheldon Gold. This thriller series has enough legal twists and fancy dancing with the law to make the great Perry Mason envious!

An Embarrassment of P.I. Riches

Lawrence Block, Loren D. Estleman, and Rob Kantner have all won four Shamus Awards from the Private Eye Writers of America.

COP TALK: GREED IS NOT GOOD

John McClane: *Why'd you have to nuke the whole building, Hans?*

Hans Gruber: *Well, when you steal $600, you can just disappear. When you steal $600 million, they will find you, unless they think you're already dead.*

—BRUCE WILLIS AS DETECTIVE JOHN MCCLANE AND ALAN RICKMAN AS HANS GRUBER IN *DIE HARD* (1988)

First Lines

"It was the end of an era, one that I suspect historians may look upon as the last decade of American innocence." —*CRUSADER'S CROSS* (2005) BY JAMES LEE BURKE

Fatal Flight

Jack Graham didn't care how many people died, as long as his mother was one of them. So he gave Daisie King a "Christmas present" to take aboard her flight from Denver on her way to Alaska. Soon after takeoff on November 1, 1955, United Airlines 629 exploded, killing all forty-four passengers and crew.

Investigators traced the bomb to Graham, a twenty-four-year-old with a record of forgery, a large amount of insurance on his mother, and a substantial inheritance coming his way. He'd previously collected insurance money by parking his car on the railroad tracks and setting a fire and explosion at his family's restaurant.

Graham's trial was the first time TV cameras were allowed in a U.S. court, with film broadcast later. He was convicted of murder and executed in January 1957.

> *"As far as feeling remorse for these people, I don't. I can't help it. Everybody pays their way and takes their chances. That's just the way it goes."*
> —JACK GRAHAM, AIRLINE BOMBER

The Joke's on Lizzie

There's a joke that's been making the rounds in Fall River, Massachusetts, for years: Lizzie Borden asked her mother if she could go to the beach. Her mother answered, "Go axe your father."

Move Over, O. J. Simpson

The Lizzie Borden murders and trial were to the late 1800s what the O. J. murders and trial were to the late 1900s. But why all the hoopla and debate about the guilt of someone who was, after all, acquitted of the crime well over 100 years ago? Maybe for the same reason there's still so much controversy swirling around the O. J. case. Most people think Lizzie did it and, as was true in the O. J. case, many feel she was found not guilty because of who she was and not what she did.

Motive: Daddy Dearest and the Wicked Stepmother

Q: What was the alleged motive for the crime with which Lizzie Borden was charged?

A: Lizzie's father, Andrew, was a cheapskate. Though he was wealthy and could certainly afford it, he refused to move the family into a classier neighborhood. He even refused to have inside plumbing. Lizzie had told friends how much she disliked her stepmother. She and her sister, Emma, never ate with Andrew and their stepmother, Abby. Abby never accepted Lizzie and Emma as her own children. She fought them in order to get what little money Andrew was willing to parcel out, and spent it on her own sisters.

Means: The Girl Means Murder

Q: How did Lizzie allegedly plan the murders?

A: Lizzie had attempted to buy prussic acid, a deadly poison, at a pharmacy the day before the murders. She didn't get it. After the murders, the head of a hatchet was found in the basement. When tested for a Discovery Channel documentary, it fit precisely into a slit made by the murder weapon on the dress Abby Borden had been wearing.

Opportunity: I Was at Home in the Barn All Day

Q: Was Lizzie physically able to commit the murders?

A: Lizzie lived there and knew the habits of the two victims. She claimed to have been in the barn at the time of her father's death, but the temperature that day was well over 100 degrees. She told a number of conflicting stories about where she had been on the property during the times of the murders.

I, the White Male Jury

Lizzie's alibi was shoddy at best. But—mostly because she was a white, thirty-two-year-old Sunday-school-teaching spinster from one the city's wealthiest families—a jury of twelve men, after deliberating for about an hour, found her not guilty of a crime they couldn't imagine her committing.

Lizzie Lives on at the Playground

Lizzie Borden took an axe
And gave her mother forty whacks.
And when she saw what she had done,
She gave her father forty-one.

Get Your Facts Straight, Schoolgirls!

There are a few factual errors in the Lizzie Borden schoolyard rhyme, but good rhymes never let facts get in their way. In the first place, sharing the mistake with the joke, the lady murdered was not her mother but her stepmother. Also, it accuses Lizzie of a crime, but she was found not guilty. And finally, the victims didn't receive forty and forty-one whacks. Lizzie's stepmother, Abby, got eighteen and her father, Andrew, eleven. But the lower numbers proved more than sufficient.

The Case of the Bloody Blue Dress

If Lizzie had, in fact, taken an axe and delivered the actual number of blows—eighteen and eleven—to her stepmother and father, then, as any modern forensic follower knows, there would have been blood spatter. A lot of blood spatter. So why no blood on Lizzie or on her clothes? A friend of Lizzie's stated that, a couple of days after the murders, she saw Lizzie burning a blue dress. Lizzie claimed it had gotten paint on it. Since some of the people at the Borden house that day said Lizzie had been wearing a blue dress, this was likely the straw that forced authorities to indict Lizzie on homicide charges.

The Naked Assailant

Still, why no blood on Lizzie herself? We're talking about hair, face, hands. *The Legend of Lizzie Borden*, a 1975 television movie, offered a solution to this conundrum. Starring Elizabeth Montgomery, she of twitching-nose *Bewitched* fame, the movie suggested that Lizzie had stripped naked before the deed. The American version of the film suggested she was naked, the European version showed a bit. After the killings, she washed the blood off in the basement, where the head of a hatchet was later found.

Bewitching Cousins

Coincidentally, and unknown to her at the time, Elizabeth Montgomery was actually the sixth cousin, once removed, of Lizzie Borden, though the earlier television series never suggested that nose-twitching Samantha ever killed anyone.

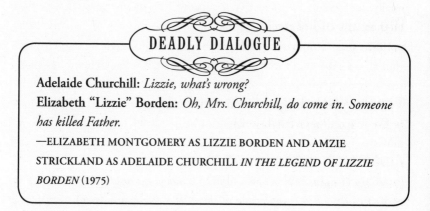

DEADLY DIALOGUE

Adelaide Churchill: *Lizzie, what's wrong?*
Elizabeth "Lizzie" Borden: *Oh, Mrs. Churchill, do come in. Someone has killed Father.*
—ELIZABETH MONTGOMERY AS LIZZIE BORDEN AND AMZIE STRICKLAND AS ADELAIDE CHURCHILL *IN THE LEGEND OF LIZZIE BORDEN* (1975)

Greedy for Lizzie

If Lizzie was, in fact, busy on a killing spree and hiding the evidence and facing down the police who arrived that August morning in 1892, it was nothing like the industry that has built up around the crime and subsequent trial.

There have been dozens of books (both fiction and nonfiction), plays, documentaries, and movies on the subject. There have been songs, a musical, a ballet, and an opera. There's even a television miniseries in the works at HBO starring Chloe Sevigny. There doesn't seem to be a video game yet but, considering the axe and blood angles, one can't be too far off.

The murder house is now a bed-and-breakfast where people claim to have seen the ghosts of Abby and Andrew wandering around. There's a "Forty Whacks" museum in Salem, Massachusetts, dedicated to the killings and trial.

100 Years of Lizzie

In 1992 there was a five-day conference that brought Lizzie fans and experts from all over the world to Fall River for a Lizzie Borden Centennial. There were twenty-eight papers presented: for, against, and unsure of Lizzie's guilt. While there were obvious strong disagreements, no one was murdered during the proceedings of that conference.

COP TALK: GREED IS NOT GOOD

Marge Gunderson: *So that was Mrs. Lundegaard on the floor in there. And I guess that was your accomplice in the wood chipper. And those three people in Brainerd. And for what? For a little bit of money. There's more to life than a little money, you know. Don'tcha know that? And here ya are, and it's a beautiful day. Well. I just don't understand it.*
—FRANCES MCDORMAND AS POLICE CHIEF MARGE GUNDERSON IN *FARGO* (1996)

"It has always seemed strange to me . . . the things we admire in men, kindness and generosity, openness, honesty, understanding and feeling, are the concomitants of failure in our system. And those traits we detest, sharpness, greed, acquisitiveness, meanness, egotism and self-interest, are the traits of success. And while men admire the quality of the first they love the produce of the second." —JOHN STEINBECK

The Quotable P.I.

Charlotte Sternwood: *Wha-? You don't want money?*

Philip Marlowe: *Oh sure. All I itch for is money. I'm so greedy that for fifty pounds a day plus expenses on the day I work, I risk my future, the hatred of the cops, of Eddie Mars and his pals, I dodge bullets and put up with slaps and say, "Thank you very much. If you have any further trouble please call me: I'll just put my card here on the table." I do all that for a few pounds. And maybe just a little bit to protect what little pride a sick and broken old man has in his family, so that he can believe his blood is not poisoned. That his little girls—though they may be a trifle wild—are not perverts and killers.* —ROBERT MITCHUM AS PHILIP MARLOWE AND SARAH MILES AS CHARLOTTE STERNWOOD IN *THE BIG SLEEP* (1978)

"But men are so full of greed today, they'll sell anything for a little piece of money." —LITTLE RICHARD

A Comedy of Murders

Match these send-ups of crimes to the comic geniuses who brought them to life, er, death:

1. *A Fish Called Wanda* (1988)	**a.** Neil Simon
2. *Murder by Death* (1999)	**b.** Jacques Rivette
3. *Manhattan Murder Mystery* (1993)	**c.** Robert Thomas
4. *Clue* (1985)	**d.** Carl Hiassen
5. *8 Women* (2002)	**e.** Susan Isaacs
6. *Celine and Julie Go Boating* (1974)	**f.** John Landis
7. *Compromising Positions* (1985)	**g.** John Cleese
8. *The Hot Rock* (1972)	**h.** Woody Allen
9. *Sick Puppy* (2000)	**i.** Donald Westlake

ANSWERS: 1-g; 2-a; 3-h; 4-f; 5-c; 6-b; 7-e; 8-i; 9-d

> "*Greed is the inventor of injustice as well as the current enforcer.*"
> —JULIAN CASABLANCAS

DEADLY DIALOGUE

Wanda Gershwitz: *[after Otto breaks in on Wanda and Archie in Archie's flat and hangs him out the window] I was dealing with something delicate, Otto. I'm setting up a guy who's incredibly important to us, who's going to tell me where the loot is and if they're going to come and arrest you. And you come loping in like Rambo without a jockstrap and you dangle him out a fifth-floor window. Now, was that smart? Was it shrewd? Was it good tactics? Or was it stupid?*

Otto West: *Don't call me stupid.*

Wanda: *Oh, right! To call you stupid would be an insult to stupid people! I've known sheep that could outwit you. I've worn dresses with higher IQs. But you think you're an intellectual, don't you, ape?*

Otto: *Apes don't read philosophy.*

Wanda: *Yes, they do, Otto. They just don't understand it. Now let me correct you on a couple of things, okay? Aristotle was not Belgian. The central message of Buddhism is not "Every man for himself." And the London Underground is not a political movement. Those are all mistakes, Otto. I looked them up.*

—JAMIE LEE CURTIS AS WANDA GERSHWITZ AND KEVIN KLINE AS OTTO WEST IN *A Fish Called Wanda* (1988)

Diamonds, Dupes, and Dead Fish

Although *A Fish Called Wanda* (1988) is more of a comedy-heist movie, it does take a very funny look at the all-too-self-important British legal system and, in particular, the priggish lifestyle of unhappily married solicitor Archie Leach (John Cleese). The unsuspecting Leach becomes a pawn in a London gang's failed jewel heist. Actually the heist itself goes off quite well until the members of the gang get greedy and double-cross each other. Beautiful and sexy gang member Wanda Gershwitz (Jamie Lee Curtis) dimes out leader of the gang Georges Thomason (Tom Georgeson) and he's arrested. Prior to his arrest, though, he had the jewels removed from the safe spot and hidden by trusted gang member and avid animal lover, the genteel gangster Ken Pile (Michael Palin). As a result of the double-cross gone bad, Wanda seduces Leach, who has been assigned as Thomason's counsel. In one hilarious stiff-upper-lip scene after another, the excessively proud Leach, to no avail, tries to squelch his lust for Wanda. And when Wanda begins to fall for Leach, in walks her jealous, angry, and rather ignorant lover, Otto West (Kevin Kline). West, a thug-bully to boot, will do whatever it takes to get the gems, including—in one sinister, gluttonous sitting—eating poor Ken's prized tropical fish. It's a delightful look at the lighter side of the British criminal justice system where the bad guys aren't so bad and the good guys not so likable.

"Looking so cool, his greed is hard to conceal, he's fresh out of law school, you gave him a license to steal." —AL STEWART

The Coroner's Gone Missing

The Marion County, Indiana, coroner's office had more than its share of problems, beginning back in 2005. Allegations arose when deputy coroner John Linehan discovered that more than $3,000 in cash and property belonging to a dead man had gone missing. Linehan said Marion County coroner Kenneth Ackles wanted the matter to be investigated internally.

"When Dr. Ackles first told me that reporting this will make him look bad, my comeback to him was, 'I think we would look bad if we didn't report it,'" Linehan said. Uh, yes.

However, in November 2006, photographs taken in the Marion County coroner's office showed that case evidence and dead people's property were being kept in the open, vulnerable to contamination or theft. The photos came two months after grand jury investigators began probing the coroner's office, checking allegations that $10,000 in cash was stolen from three bodies.

The Quotable P.I. _____

Loren Visser: *Well, if the pay's right and it's legal, I'll do it.*

Julian Marty: *It's not strictly legal.*

Visser: *Well, if the pay's right, I'll do it.*

—M. EMMET WALSH AS P.I. LOREN VISSER AND DAN HEDAYA AS JULIAN MARTY IN *BLOOD SIMPLE* (1984)

"Greed is a bottomless pit which exhausts the person in an endless effort to satisfy the need without ever reaching satisfaction." —ERICH FROMM

Oops, I've Been Cremated!

In June 2006, relatives of Carl Southern reported him missing. Months later, they learned that not only was he dead, but that his remains had been cremated—and that the Marion County coroner's office had identified the body weeks before, but failed to tell them or police.

SLOTH

n., from the Middle English *slowth,* meaning slow

1. Laziness, apathy, and disinclination in regard to virtue
2. Slow-moving mammals from the family Bradypodidae found in South and Central America
3. A group of bears

"You must avoid sloth, that wicked siren." —**HORACE**

Conventional wisdom has it that criminals by definition take the easy way out—every crime is at some level the lazy approach to a problem. But the sloth of the criminal class is often compounded by indolence and incompetence on the part of law enforcement and the criminal justice system—to murderous result.

> *"I don't think necessity is the mother of invention. Invention, in my opinion, arises directly from idleness, possibly also from laziness—to save oneself trouble."* —AGATHA CHRISTIE

Stranger Than Fiction

Q: Name one real-life case of spectacularly unimaginative problem-solving connected to Theodore Dreiser's novel, *An American Tragedy* (1925).

A: In 1906, Chester Gillette was convicted of killing his pregnant, lower-class girlfriend, Grace Brown, during a row on Big Moose Lake in the Adirondacks. Dreiser saved news clippings on the case and almost twenty years later published his novel, in which he even gave the main character, Clyde Griffiths, the same initials as Gillette.

> *"Did she think as she gathered those flowers*
> *That grew on the shores of the lake,*
> *That the hand that plucked those sweet lilies*
> *Her own sweet life they would take?"*
> —BALLAD "THE MURDER OF GRACE BROWN"

Never Swim at Night

If Grace Brown's murder inspired *An American Tragedy*, Freda McKechnie's murder may have been inspired by it. In 1934, another promising young man was accused of killing his pregnant girlfriend, Freda McKechnie, a telephone operator, during a nocturnal swim at Harveys Lake in Pennsylvania. Robert Allan Edwards was convicted of Freda's murder, in part because of the love letters he had written to another woman, music teacher Margaret Crain. The case was dubbed "The American Tragedy Murder" by the press, and

the *New York Post* sent a special correspondent to cover the trial—Theodore
Dreiser.

First Lines

*"Hamish Macbeth did not like change, although this was something he
would not even admit to himself, preferring to think of himself as a go-
ahead, modern man."*—*DEATH OF A CELEBRITY* (2002) BY M. C. BEATON

P.I. Writers Take Note

"Writer's block? That's just another word for 'lazy.'"—ROBERT B. PARKER
(WHO PUBLISHED SIXTY-NINE NOVELS BETWEEN 1972 AND 2011,
THIRTY-NINE FEATURING P.I. SPENSER AND SIX FEATURING P.I. SUNNY
RANDALL)

If You Only Write One Book . . .

To Kill a Mockingbird (1960) has sold more than 150 million copies. The
novel remains a cornerstone classic of American literature still read in school-
rooms all over the nation.

*"If you just learn a single trick, Scout, you'll get along a lot better with
all kinds of folks. You never really understand a person until you consider
things from his point of view. . . . Until you climb inside of his skin and
walk around in it."*—GREGORY PECK AS ATTICUS FINCH IN *TO KILL A
MOCKINGBIRD* (1962)

Get Off That Couch and Become a P.I.

There's no better time to become a private investigator. Here's why:

"Employment of private detectives and investigators is expected to grow 22 percent over the 2008—2018 decade, much faster than the average for all occupations.

"Private detectives and investigators held about 45,500 jobs in 2008. About 21 percent were self-employed, including many for whom investigative work was a second job. Around 41 percent of detective and investigator jobs were in investigation and security services, including private detective agencies. The rest worked mostly in State and local government, legal services firms, department or other general merchandise stores, employment services companies, insurance agencies, and credit mediation establishments, including banks and other depository institutions."

—*OCCUPATIONAL OUTLOOK HANDBOOK, 2010–11 EDITION,* BUREAU OF LABOR STATISTICS

Don't Call These Private Investigators Lazy

Not only were these people P.I.s in real life, they wrote about fictional P.I.s. Match the real-life private investigator to his or her creation:

1. Kelley Kavenaugh, *Hard Impact* (2004)
2. Art Hardin, *Private Heat* (2002)
3. Cal Brantley, *The Losers' Club* (2000)
4. Lucien Caye, *New Orleans Confidential* (2006)
5. Joop Wheeler, "And Maybe the Horse Will Learn to Sing" (*Alfred Hitchcock Mystery Magazine*, 1998)
6. Diana Hunter, *Old Poison* (2003)
7. Lupe Solano, *Bloody Waters* (1996)
8. Dan Kearney & Associates, *Dead Skip* (1972)
9. Stanley Hastings, *Detective* (1987)
10. The Continental Op, *Red Harvest* (1929); Sam Spade, *The Maltese Falcon* (1930); and Nick and Nora Charles, *The Thin Man* (1934)
11. Devon MacDonald, *The Turquoise Tattoo* (1991)
12. Nick Polo, *Polo Solo* (1987)
13. Nick Merchant, *The Heir Hunter* (2000)
14. Nell Fury, *The Two-Bit Tango* (1992)
15. Streeter, *The Low End of Nowhere* (1997)
16. Cecil Younger, *The Woman Who Married a Bear* (1992)
17. Paulina Stewart, *This Little Baby* (1997)
18. Neal Carey, *A Cool Breeze on the Underground* (1991)

a. Jerry Kennealy
b. O'Neil De Noux
c. Carolina Garcia-Aguilera
d. Chris Larsgaard
e. Robert E. Bailey
f. Joan Francis
g. Joyce Sullivan
h. Susan Andrews
i. Elizabeth Pincus
j. Joe Gores
k. Lise S. Baker
l. John Straley
m. Nancy Baker Jacobs
n. Don Winslow
o. Greg Fallis
p. Parnell Hall
q. Michael Stone
r. Dashiell Hammett

ANSWERS: 1-h; 2-e; 3-k; 4-b; 5-o; 6-f; 7-c; 8-j; 9-p; 10-r; 11-m; 12-a; 13-d; 14-i; 15-q; 16-l; 17-g; 18-n

❧ *First Lines*

"I got to the office early that morning—I think it was about ten o'clock."
—*FLOOD* (1985) BY ANDREW VACHSS

The Hardest-Working Cop Portrayals on TV

The people behind the following shows didn't cut corners when it came to research. These are among the most authentic representations of police work to ever air on television.

- *Dragnet* (1952–1959; 1967–1970)
- *Adam-12* (1968–1975)
- *Police Story* (1973–1977)
- *Barney Miller* (1974–1982)
- *Hill Street Blues* (1981–1987)
- *Law & Order* (1990– 2010)
- *Homicide: Life on the Street* (1993–1999)
- *NYPD Blue* (1993–2005)
- *The Wire* (2002–2008)

Anything But a Sloth

The "Police Writers" website lists 214 active and retired police officers who also write about fictional cops. (Those would be the ones who are around when you need them?)

AKA Workhorse

Between 1956 (*Cop Hater*) and 2005 (*Fiddlers*), Ed McBain published fifty-four novels in the 87th Precinct series. If you add in his many pseudonyms (D. A. Addams, Curt Cannon, Hunt Collins, Evan Hunter, S. A. Lombino,

Richard Marsten, and Ted Taine), the man originally born as Salvatore Albert Lombino published well over 100 novels.

Now that's some rap sheet.

Lazy . . . Or Something Else Entirely?

The popular realm of police stories (whether fiction, television, or film) can be separated by *modus operandi*:

- Police procedurals are marked by a realistic portrayal of police procedures and cop-shop culture.
- Nonprocedurals aren't.

Messages Left on Jim Rockford's Answering Machine

"This is Jim Rockford. At the tone, leave your name and message. I'll get back to you."

"It's Norma at the market. It bounced. You want me to tear it up, send it back, or put it with the others?" —EPISODE 101, 09-13-1974, "THE KIRKOFF CASE," *THE ROCKFORD FILES*

"This is the phone company. I see you're using our unit, now how about paying for it?" —EPISODE 109, 11-08-1974, "IN PURSUIT OF CAROL THORNE," *THE ROCKFORD FILES*

"This is Mrs. Moseley at the library. We billed you for your overdue book Karate Made Easy. *We abuse our library, we don't get our cards renewed."* —EPISODE 113, 12-27-1974, "PROFIT AND LOSS, PART 2: LOSS," *THE ROCKFORD FILES*

> *"Sonny, this is Dad. Never mind giving that talk on your occupation to the Gray Power Club. Hap Dudley's son is a doctor and everybody'd sorta ... well, rather hear from him, but thanks."* —EPISODE 421-2, 02-24-1978, "THE HOUSE ON WILLIS AVENUE, PART II," *THE ROCKFORD FILES*

The Quotable P.I.

Ezekiel Rawlins: *A man once told me that you step out of your door in the morning, and you are already in trouble.* —DENZEL WASHINGTON AS P.I. EZEKIEL "EASY" RAWLINS IN *DEVIL IN A BLUE DRESS* (1995)

✎ First Lines

"Gowan Kilbride, aged sixteen, had never been much for early rising. While still living on his parents' farm, he had grumbled his way out of bed each morning, letting everyone within hearing distance know, through a variety of groans and created complaints, how little to his liking the life of husbandry was." —*PAYMENT IN BLOOD* (1989) BY ELIZABETH GEORGE

The Lamest Cops on TV

Don't think you can sail through the academy by watching the following "masters" of law enforcement.

- Lieutenant Jim Dangle of *Reno 911* (2003–2009)
- Sergeant Frank Drebin, Detective Lieutenant, *Police Squad!* (1982)
- Deputy Sheriff Barney Fife, *The Andy Griffith Show* (1960–1968)
- Sheriff Rosco P. Coltrane, *The Dukes of Hazzard* (1979–1985)
- The Entire Cast of *Cop Rock* (1990)

KILLER WIT

"If I were to make another picture set in Australia, I'd have a policeman hop into the pocket of a kangaroo and yell, 'Follow that car!'"
—ALFRED HITCHCOCK

◎ First Lines

"A grey bird glided in and out of Harry's field of vision. He drummed his fingers on the steering wheel. Slow time. Somebody had been talking about 'slow time' on TV yesterday. This was slow time. Like on Christmas Eve before Father Christmas came. Or sitting in the electric chair before the current was turned on." —THE REDBREAST (2007) BY JO NESBØ

COP TALK: HARD AT WORK

Harry Callahan: *Everybody wants results but nobody wants to do what they have to do to get them done.*
—CLINT EASTWOOD AS DIRTY HARRY CALLAHAN IN *SUDDEN IMPACT* (1983)

Blood Simple

They say blood will tell. Though O. J. Simpson was acquitted on charges that he had murdered his wife, Nicole Brown Simpson, and her friend Ronald Goldman, blood told a different story. It was everywhere, screaming for attention. At the crime scene at the Bundy Drive premises, Simpson's blood was found at the exact spot where the murders were committed. The walk and the rear gate at the crime scene had blood from Simpson. This was determined by using genetic fingerprinting. A trail of blood was found at the crime scene as well as in Simpson's white Bronco and at his house. Tests show that three stains on the Bronco's console were a mixture of O. J.'s blood with that of both victims. Another console stain was a mixture of O. J.'s and Ron's blood. Nicole's blood was found on the driver's side carpet. Drops of O. J.'s blood led from his driveway into the foyer of his Rockingham mansion. Blood on socks in O. J.'s bedroom matched O. J.'s and Nicole's. Police found blood in the shower and sink of O. J.'s bathroom after the murders.

The Three Stooges versus O. J. Simpson

If the forensics in the case were doing so much heavy lifting, how did O. J. get acquitted? The prosecution of the O. J. murder trial, one of the most famous and obsessively followed cases ever, was marred throughout by careless, maybe even lazy police work. Simpson's stellar defense team managed to present the investigation of the crime as a Hollywood production that was more "Three Stooges" than "Preserve and Protect."

Slapstick Forensics 101: The Intern

One of the items the defense insisted had not been well-preserved was the vial containing Simpson's blood sample. It was revealed that the police scientist who collected blood samples from Simpson to compare with evidence from the crime scene was a trainee. She carried the vial around in her lab coat pocket for most of the day before relinquishing it as an exhibit.

> *"I haven't gone out and actively tried to pursue any work."* —O. J. SIMPSON TO KATIE COURIC IN A 2004 INTERVIEW, TEN YEARS AFTER THE MURDER TRIAL

Slapstick Forensics 101: The Cop

Then, of course, there was Detective Mark Fuhrman, who, the defense alleged, had framed O. J. by planting some of the evidence. Fuhrman insisted he was not a racist. He said he had not used the n-word to describe black people in the past ten years. An audiotape of his being interviewed a few years earlier, however, had him using that word forty-one times.

> *"Stop being angry. You participated in the failure. You did nothing creative. You did nothing to stop this."* —DETECTIVE MARK FUHRMAN, IN REFERENCE TO SIMPSON MURDER TRIAL PROSECUTING ATTORNEY CHRIS DARDEN, FIFTEEN YEARS AFTER THE VERDICT, ON *OPRAH*

Slapstick Forensics 101: The Glove

And finally, there was the infamous bloody glove, found near the guest-house where Kato Kaelin was staying on Simpson's estate. It was a match to the glove found at the murder scene. Simpson's wife had bought him two pairs of the gloves a few years earlier. The prosecution stated that both gloves contained DNA from Simpson as well as the two victims. The defense argued that Mark Fuhrman had likely planted it there. Chief prosecutor Marcia Clark and others had told assistant prosecutor Christopher Darden not to have Simpson try on the glove. It had been blood-soaked. It had been frozen and unfrozen a number of times. But he asked anyway. And the rest is history.

> *"If it doesn't fit, you must acquit."* —JOHNNY COCHRAN, O. J. SIMPSON'S ATTORNEY

The Odds of Guilt

DNA tests proved that in at least one blood drop found at the Bundy Drive murder scene, the chances of it belonging to anyone but O. J. were about 170 million to one. Just on the blood evidence alone, there was only one out of 57 billion chances that Simpson was innocent. Fifty-seven billion is almost ten times the population of the world.

BLOOD & BONES

"A cartridge case at the scene of offence could prove as incriminating as if the murderer had left his visiting card!" —SIR SYDNEY SMITH

"I didn't do the crime. I'm not going to pay them a dime. And that's the name of that tune, you know." —O. J. SIMPSON

The Circle of Crime

On the night of September 13, 2007, a group of men led by O. J. Simpson entered a hotel room in Las Vegas and left with Simpson sports memorabilia. According to Bruce Fromong, a self-described former sports memorabilia dealer and the first witness in Simpson's preliminary hearing, a group of men broke into his room and stole the Simpson memorabilia at gunpoint.

Three days later, on September 16, Simpson was arrested for his involvement in the robbery and held without bail. He admitted taking the items, which he said had been stolen from him, but denied breaking into the room. Simpson also denied the allegation that he or the people with him carried guns.

> *"I'm O. J. Simpson. How am I going to think that I'm going to rob some-*
> *body and get away with it? Besides, I thought what happens in Las Vegas*
> *stays in Las Vegas."* —O. J. SIMPSON

Thirteen Was His Unlucky Number

On October 3, 2008, Simpson was found guilty of all twelve charges, exactly thirteen years to the day after he was acquitted of the murders of his wife, Nicole, and Ronald Goldman. On December 5, 2008, Simpson was sentenced to thirty-three years in prison while eligible for parole in nine years.

Murder by Rhyme

> *"Murder may pass unpunish'd for a time,*
> *But tardy justice will o'ertake the crime."* —JOHN DRYDEN, *COCK AND*
> *THE FOX* (1700)

☙ *First Lines*

"I hate running errands. I put them off and put them off, and then one morning the cat's got no food, there are zero stamps on the roll, and I realize I own no underwear minus holes." —*DEEP POCKETS* (2004) BY LINDA BARNES

Why Every P.I. Needs a Sidekick

When the cops fail to produce results, people call on the private investigators. When the private investigators reach lines they don't want to cross, they call on the sidekicks. Match the sidekick to the gumshoe and creator.

1. Hawk
2. Raymond "Mouse" Alexander
3. Bubba Rogowski

4. Joe Pike
5. Windsor "Win" Lockwood

a. Easy Rawlins (Walter Mosley)
b. Patrick Kenzie and Angela Gennaro (Dennis Lehane)
c. Myron Bolitar (Harlan Coben)
d. Elvis Cole (Robert Crais)
e. Spenser (Robert B. Parker)

ANSWERS: 1-e; 2-a; 3-b; 4-d; 5-c

The Quotable P.I.

"When a man's partner is killed, he's supposed to do something about it. It doesn't make any difference what you thought of him. He was your partner and you're supposed to do something about it." —HUMPHREY BOGART AS P.I. SAM SPADE IN *THE MALTESE FALCON* (1941)

I Have People Who Do That

Nero Wolfe (Rex Stout) is so lazy that he sends his assistant, Archie Goodwin, out to do all the investigative work.

◈ First Lines

"When I finally caught up with Abraham Trahearne, he was drinking beer with an alcoholic bulldog named Fireball Roberts in a ramshackle joint just outside of Sonoma, California, drinking the heart right out of a fine spring afternoon." —THE LAST GOOD KISS (1978) BY JAMES CRUMLEY

Disorganized in Death

Some killers give the impression they didn't set out to hurt anybody; they just couldn't resist the opportunity. They seize victims by chance, sometimes at risk to themselves. They use whatever weapons or bindings are at hand. They leave the bodies behind or with minimal concealment and often provide a wealth of forensic evidence for investigators, too. They are often of low intelligence or poorly educated, lacking in self-esteem and basic social skills. They attack suddenly and viciously, driven by the need to overpower their victims.

Disorganized Offenders of (Messy) Note

Killers with this type of "disorganized offender" behavior include:

- Ed Gein
- Juan Corona
- "The Vampire of Sacramento" AKA Richard Trenton Chase
- Aileen Wuornos, one of the rare female sexual serial killers

Get Organized with a Murder Kit

Other killers seem to plan everything down to the smallest detail. They carefully select their victims, plan their method of approach, carry a "murder kit," and are skilled at whisking away their victims and hiding the bodies. They are often bright, even charming, guys who blend into the social scene. In actuality, they are sadistic liars and manipulators who need to exert absolute control over their victims and the circumstances of their crimes.

Organized Offenders of (Neat) Notes

Killers who displayed this type of "organized offender" behavior include:

- Edmund Kemper
- John Wayne Gacy
- Kenneth Bianchi and Angelo Buono, AKA The Hillside Stranglers

Ted Bundy: Organized or Disorganized?

Both. Life is messy and so is murder. Apparently there is no either-or division of killer behavior or personality types. Killers may display a mixture of characteristics or evolve over time. Ted Bundy was the quintessential "organized offender" up through his murder conviction in Colorado, but his last brutal murders after he escaped to Florida were "disorganized" in nature.

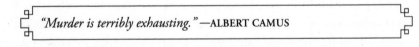

"Murder is terribly exhausting." —ALBERT CAMUS

Next Time You Decide to Kill Someone, Don't Plan Ahead!

"The boys with their feet on the desks know that the easiest murder case in the world to break is the one somebody tried to get very cute with; the one that really bothers them is the murder somebody only thought of two minutes before he pulled it off." —RAYMOND CHANDLER (WHO COAUTHORED THE SCREENPLAY BASED ON JAMES M. CAIN'S *DOUBLE INDEMNITY*, IN WHICH THE KILLERS TRIED TOO HARD)

"You know you're reading a great mystery novel when you're up at three in the morning, unable to put it down. When you finally fall asleep, the characters go romping around in your dreams. When you get to the final page, you smack yourself in the head because the solution seems obvious in retrospect yet came as a complete surprise." —*WRITING AND SELLING YOUR MYSTERY NOVEL* (2005) BY HALLIE EPHRON

Stumped by Perry Mason

Would you believe that America's favorite lawyer of all time, Perry Mason, never cracked any of his cases? Well . . . sort of. Raymond Burr, who played Perry Mason in the enormously successful TV series from 1957–1966 in some 271 episodes and then again from 1985–1993, said that he never managed to solve any of the cases until he'd read them all through. In fact, he admitted further that he'd often been puzzled about who committed the murder even after shooting the script. Sounds like The Case of the Slothful Thespian.

Q: When did Raymond Burr, TV's most famous defense attorney, play a murderer?

A: Burr played bad guy Lars Thorwald in the Hitchcock classic *Rear Window* (1954), starring Jimmy Stewart and Grace Kelly.

Producing Is Murder

Rumor has it that director Alfred Hitchcock chose Burr to play the killer in *Rear Window*, because Burr looked like David O. Selznick. Selznick drove Hitchcock crazy with what the legendary director saw as too much meddling in his films.

KILLER WIT

"Then, Madam, I suggest you have her dry cleaned."

—ALFRED HITCHCOCK, TO THE WOMAN WHO COMPLAINED THAT *PSYCHO'S* SHOWER SCENE SO FRIGHTENED HER DAUGHTER THAT THE GIRL WOULD NO LONGER SHOWER

◌ First Lines

"Between the hot flashes, the hangover, and all the spam on my computer, there's no way I'll get anything done before eight o'clock this morning."

—*PRIME TIME* (2007) BY HANK PHILLIPPI RYAN

Whom Can You Trust—in the Bible?

In one of the most celebrated biblical murders, the leader of the mighty Canaanite army survived the battle in which his forces were annihilated, only to be killed by the woman he trusted to hide him from his pursuers (Judges 4 & 5). Sisera commanded a force of "nine hundred iron chariots" that oppressed the Israelites for twenty years until the great prophetess and judge Deborah persuaded Barak to lead a force of ten thousand men against him. She promised Barak victory, but said Sisera himself would be delivered into the power of a woman.

Sure enough, the defeated general fled the battlefield for friendly territory and stumbled into the tent of a woman whose sympathies were with the Israelites. Jael (or Yael) welcomed Sisera with promises that he would be safe and made a fuss over him. She gave him milk to drink when he asked for water, covered him over with a rug, and agreed to stand guard while he slept. Sisera relaxed his defenses and fell into an exhausted sleep.

Then, Says the Song of Deborah:

> *"Her hand reached for the tent peg, her right hand for the workman's hammer. She struck Sisera, she crushed his head, she shattered and pierced his temple."* —JUDGES 5:26 NIV

Yael Bloody Murder(er)

When Barak and his soldiers came looking for Sisera, Jael showed them his dead body in her tent.

Just Call Her Hammerhead Yael

Yael is one of the most popular names for girls in Israel.

> *"There are only about twenty murders a year in London and not all are serious—some are just husbands killing their wives."* —COMMANDER G. H. HATHERILL, SCOTLAND YARD, 1954

First Lines
"It was one hell of a night to throw away a baby." —IN THE BLEAK MIDWINTER (2003) BY JULIA SPENCER-FLEMING

Fickle Finger-Pointing of Fate
In 1989, Charles Stuart of Boston said he and his wife, Carol, were shot by a black man who forced his way into their car when they were driving home from childbirth class. Though gravely wounded himself, it turned out Stuart had staged the shootings that killed Carol and their baby, Christopher. He didn't want to change his lifestyle to accommodate a baby and the loss of Carol's income. Before he could be arrested, he jumped off a bridge to his death.

> *"A murderer is regarded by the conventional world as something almost monstrous, but a murderer to himself is only an ordinary man. It is only if the murderer is a good man that he can be regarded as monstrous."*
> —GRAHAM GREENE

First Lines
"This is a sampler of murder, hopefully designed not only for the aficionado but for the readers who have hitherto paid little attention to accounts of murder outside of fiction." —THE QUALITY OF MURDER: 300 YEARS OF TRUE CRIME (1962) EDITED BY ANTHONY BOUCHER

Who, Me?
If you're going to get stabbed or have a heart attack, don't do it in a crowd. Psychologists say the chances of any one person coming to your aid go down the more people there are around. They all figure somebody else is calling

911 or somebody else is a doctor, a nurse, an EMT, or an Eagle Scout. "These other folks aren't doing anything; no need for me to get involved, either."

> *"Some men are alive simply because it is against the law to kill them."*
> —EDGAR WATSON HOWE

First Lines

"I was nursing a bottle of Murphy's Irish Whiskey, drinking it from the neck of the bottle sparingly, and looking down from the window of my office at Berkeley Street where it crosses Boylston." —THE WIDENING GYRE (1983) BY ROBERT B. PARKER

Stand by for Murder

The first studies of the "bystander effect" were prompted by the 1964 stabbing death and rape of Catherine "Kitty" Genovese in Queens, New York. Exaggerated reports at that time claimed that thirty-eight neighbors had witnessed the assault over a period of thirty-five minutes and did nothing. The less spectacular, but still chilling, truth is that at least a dozen people heard Kitty's cries for help when she was first stabbed outside her apartment building at 3:15 A.M. Most said later they thought it was the usual rowdiness from the neighboring bar or a lovers' quarrel. A few admitted, "I didn't want to get involved."

The assailant actually ran away when one witness opened his window and yelled, "Leave that girl alone!" The witness then closed his window and turned out the light. Kitty was able to stagger around to the back entrance of the building (which may have led some witnesses to believe she wasn't badly hurt), but could not get through the inner door. Her killer returned to look for her, raped her, and stabbed her repeatedly. A witness to the final assault called the police, but Kitty died in the ambulance.

COP TALK: HARD AT WORK

Deputy Bill Geisler: *I don't know about Ray, but not everyone in Garrison is a murderer.*

Sheriff Freddy Heflin: *No, they just keep their eyes closed and their mouths shut, just like me.*

—SYLVESTER STALLONE AS SHERIFF FREDDY HEFLIN AND NOAH EMMERICH AS DEPUTY BILL GEISLER IN *COP LAND* (1997)

The Good Samaritan—Not!

The bystander effect is also known as "Genovese syndrome."

COP TALK: HARD AT WORK

William Somerset: *I just don't think I can continue to live in a place that embraces and nurtures apathy as if it was virtue.*

David Mills: *You're no different. You're no better.*

William Somerset: *I didn't say I was different or better. I'm not. Hell, I sympathize; I sympathize completely. Apathy is the solution. I mean, it's easier to lose yourself in drugs than it is to cope with life. It's easier to steal what you want than it is to earn it. It's easier to beat a child than it is to raise it. Hell, love costs: it takes effort and work.*

—BRAD PITT AS DETECTIVE DAVID MILLS AND MORGAN FREEMAN AS DETECTIVE LIEUTENANT WILLIAM SOMERSET IN *SE7EN* (1995)

Merry Christmas to Murder

On Christmas Day in 1974, a twenty-five-year-old model named Sandra Zahler was beaten to death in her apartment, ironically in the same Queens neighborhood where Kitty Genovese died. One report also said her dog's leg was broken. Neighbors heard banging and screams from Zahler's apartment, but did nothing. Her ex-boyfriend surrendered to police a week later.

> *"Nothing irritates me more than chronic laziness in others. Mind you, it's only mental sloth I object to. Physical sloth can be heavenly."*
> —ELIZABETH HURLEY

Hit in Hartford

In May 2008, a seventy-eight-year-old man named Angel Arce Torres was struck by a hit-and-run driver on a busy street in Hartford, Connecticut. Video from a streetlight surveillance camera showed cars continuing to drive by the man lying in the street and pedestrians either looking on from a distance or going about their business. Four calls were made to 911, but no one approached the victim until a police car responding to an unrelated call pulled up at the scene. Torres was paralyzed and died, still in the hospital, a year later.

> *"Sloth and Silence are a Fool's Virtues."* —BENJAMIN FRANKLIN

Snap This Victim!

In April 2010, back in Queens again, a man was stabbed while trying to help a woman being confronted by a man with a knife. The assailant and the woman ran off, leaving thirty-one-year-old Hugo Tale-Yax bleeding on the sidewalk. Surveillance video showed people walking by the dying man for more than an hour. One man stopped to take a picture with his cell phone. Another actually rolled Tale-Yax over, saw the pool of blood, and walked on. The police were called one hour and forty minutes after the attack. By then, Tale-Yax was dead.

The Quotable P.I.

Philip Marlowe: *It was one of those transient motels, something between a fleabag and a dive.* —ROBERT MITCHUM AS P.I. PHILIP MARLOWE IN *FAREWELL, MY LOVELY* (1975)

"Murder in the murderer is no such ruinous thought as poets and romancers will have it; it does not unsettle him, or fright him from his ordinary notice of trifles: it is an act quite easy to be contemplated, but in its sequel, it turns out to be a horrible jangle and confounding of all relations."
—RALPH WALDO EMERSON

Booked for Murder

- *Armed and Dangerous: A Writer's Guide to Weapons* (1990) by Michael Newton
- *Homicide Investigation, 3rd Edition: Practical Information for Coroners, Police Officers, and Other Investigators* (1977) by LeMoyne Snyder
- *The Modern Sherlock Holmes: Introduction to Forensic Science Today* (1991) by Judy Williams
- *The Bone Detectives: How Forensic Anthropologists Solve Crimes and Uncover Mysteries of the Dead* (2001) by Donna M. Jackson

KILLER WIT

"Someone once told me that every minute a murder occurs, so I don't want to waste your time, I know you want to go back to work."
—ALFRED HITCHCOCK

First Lines

"Of all the run-down, flea-bitten Private Investigator offices in all the UK, he had to walk into mine." —*GO TO HELENA HANDBASKET* (2006) BY DONNA MOORE

They Got It on Tape

In 1976, T. Cullen Davis, a very wealthy Texas oilman, was acquitted of the murders of his estranged wife, Priscilla, her boyfriend, and her twelve-year-old daughter from a previous marriage. It was the most expensive trial to date in Texas.

Fast-Forward to the FBI

Three years later, Davis was back in court, this time for allegedly hiring one of his salesmen, David McCrory, to kill Priscilla and the judge overseeing their still drawn-out divorce proceedings. The strongest evidence against Davis was an FBI tape recording of Davis telling McCrory to kill both. Rather than convicting Davis, however, the recording actually was a key to his acquittal.

Tape-Doctoring for Dummies

The defense brought in an expert witness, Dr. Richard Shuy, a professor of linguistics at Georgetown University. Shuy testified that, after repeated listening to the tape, it was clear from the tape's odd pacing, timing, and the intonation of some of Davis's responses that Davis and McCrory were actually engaged in separate conversations. During part of the discussion, Davis had left the car the two were in and gone to the trunk, but carried on the conversation he had begun. During this time McCrory, who had been encouraged by the FBI to get Davis to admit they had a hit man arrangement, slipped in some of the more telling questions in a quiet voice that Davis most likely couldn't even hear.

As Shakespeare would have said, the prosecution was "hoisted by their own petard." It was the first time forensic discourse analysis had been used in a court case and led directly to a jury finding of not guilty.

☙ First Lines

"On the last night of August, Tess Monaghan went to the drugstore and bought a composition book—one with a black-and-white marble cover. She had done this every fall since she was six and saw no reason to change, despite the differences wrought by twenty-three years." —*BALTIMORE BLUES* (1997) BY LAURA LIPPMAN

Ten Forensic Writers and First Lines of Their Novels

In alphabetical order, ten mystery writers with forensics in their blood—or in the blood they're inspecting. Match them with the opening lines of their novels.

1. Jefferson Bass
(*Flesh and Bone*, 2007)

a. On the sixteenth of October, shadowy deer crept to the edge of the woods beyond my window as the sun peeked over the cover of the night. Plumbing above and below me groaned and one by one other rooms went bright as sharp tattoos from ranges I could not see riddled the dawn. I had gone to sleep and gotten up to the sound of gunfire.

2. Simon Beckett
(*The Chemistry of Death*, 2007)

b. A scalpel is a beautiful thing.

3. Patricia Cornwell
(*The Body Farm*, 2004)

c. Even before it all went bad she had the feeling it was going to be a rotten day.

4. Jeffery Deaver (*Edge*, 2010)

d. The chain-link gate yowled like an angry tomcat in the watery light of dawn.

5. Kathryn Fox (*Bloodborn*, 2009)

e. "Dancing Queen" Sara Linton mumbled with the music as she made her way around the skating rink. "Young and sweet, only seventeen."

6. Tess Gerritsen
(*Life Support*, 1997)

7. Kathy Reichs
(*Déjà Dead*, 1997)

8. Ruth Rendell
(*A Judgment in Stone*, 2000)

9. Jonathan Santlofer
(*The Death Artist*, 2002)

10. Karin Slaughter
(*Kisscut*, 2002)

f. Eunice Parchman killed the Coverdale family because she could not read or write.

g. A human body starts to decompose four minutes after death. Once the encapsulation of life, it now undergoes its final metamorphosis.

h. The man who wanted to kill the young woman sitting beside me was three-quarters of a mile behind us as we drove through a pastoral setting of tobacco and cotton fields this humid morning.

i. I wasn't thinking about the man who had blown himself up. Earlier I had. Now I was putting him together.

j. Doctor Anna Chrichton prepared to face the violent offenders. Hundreds of thousands of taxpayers' dollars had gone into the trial and now retrial of the four whose heinous crimes had horrified even the most jaded police and lawyers.

ANSWERS: 1-d; 2-g; 3-a; 4-h; 5-j; 6-b; 7-i; 8-f; 9-c; 10-e

First Lines

"That Sunday, the sun floated bright and hot over the Los Angeles basin, pushing people to the beaches and the parks and into backyard pools to escape the heat." —*L.A. REQUIEM* (1999) **BY ROBERT CRAIS**

Lazy Does It

1. Who gave us his take of the court system in *The Ways of the Hour*, published in 1850?
2. Who introduced legal loopholer attorney Randolph Mason in the 1896 collection of short stories titled, *The Strange Schemes of Randolph Mason*?
3. Which pulp writer, turned bestselling creator of Nero Wolfe, published the 20,000-word legal novella *Justice Ends at Home* in *All-Story* magazine?

ANSWERS: 1) James Fenimore Cooper; 2) Melville Davisson Post; 3) Rex Stout, whose 1915 story features lazy, slow-witted, yet likable-lawyer Simon Leg.

KILLER WIT

"There is no terror in the bang, only in the anticipation of it."
—ALFRED HITCHCOCK

Cher Goes to Court

In *Suspect* (1987), the Academy-Award–winning actress plays a court-appointed defense attorney. Kathleen Riley is appointed counsel to a homeless man named Carl Wayne Anderson (Liam Neeson) who is charged with murder. During jury deliberations Riley selects reluctant juror Eddie Sanger (Dennis Quaid). Sanger, a playboy lobbyist, is at first a bit disgruntled at having to do his civic duty. Soon, however, he becomes a reluctant detective, sharing his findings with Riley.

The Truth Will Out—with a Little Help

Riley is at first shocked that Sanger would create the obvious conflict between juror and defense counsel, but ultimately the truth is more important to her than her profession. Little by little Riley and Sanger unravel a mystery reeking of old blood, greed, pride, and ambition.

> *"I spend all of my day with murderers and rapists, and what's really crazy, I like them."* —CHER AS KATHLEEN RILEY IN *SUSPECT* (1987)

The "I Hate to Lawyer" Lawyer

Rex Stout's Simon Leg doesn't like to practice law. In fact, he spends his days in his office engaged in pleasure reading, refusing to take on any cases. Much to his shock, he is called before the bench by Judge Fraser Manton and ordered to defend William Mount for the murder of his wife. Leg believes in his client's innocence, yet has no idea how to win an acquittal. His sloth has caught up with him—or has it?

> *"All men kill the thing they hate, too, unless, of course, it kills them first."* —JAMES THURBER

Everything Unjust Is New Again

Q: Which Michael Connelly novel echoes Rex Stout's novella, *Justice Ends at Home*, in theme and plot?

A: *The Brass Verdict*. Much like Mickey Haller in Michael Connelly's brilliant novel, published nearly a century after *Justice Ends at Home*, Leg has a hunch and it pays off, bringing the real killer to justice. In 1977 *Justice Ends at Home* was republished in book volume under its own title along with many of Stout's other pulp stories.

Get Off Your Duff and Solve Another Murder!

Is solving a murder really all that loathsome? Amateur detective-barrister Francis Pettigrew thinks so. Pettigrew is a reluctant detective who appears in five novels at the skillful hand of English judge and barrister Cyril Hare–a pseudonym of Arthur Alexander Gordon Clark. Hare is considered to be one of the most talented practitioners of crime literature, offering not only great characters and storytelling in the Pettigrew novels, but not surprisingly, a keen observation of the legal process as well.

Murder Magnet

While Pettigrew may appear a bit slothful when it comes to expending his energies on solving a murder (he says he "loathes the business of detection"), it's not really the case. He just wants to live a productive yet uncomplicated life—to be the kind of barrister who can go on "holiday" and enjoy it. It seems, however, external forces conspire against such notions. Wherever Pettigrew goes bodies turn up, whether it's at the sleepy government office or the English countryside.

> *"Laziness may appear attractive, but work gives satisfaction."* —ANNE FRANK

The First of Many Bodies to Come

Q: When and where did Cyril Hare's Francis Pettigrew first appear in print?

A: Pettigrew came on the scene in 1942 with the publication of *Tragedy at Law*, a book praised as a "masterpiece" by that master himself of all things erudite, Jacques Barzun.

Pettigrew's Canon

The other Pettigrew novels include:

- *With a Bare Bodkin* (1946)
- *When the Wind Blows* (1949)
- *That Yew Tree's Shade* (1954)
- *He Should Have Died Hereafter* (1957)

Seersucker Law

Why would murderers ever take up trade in Atlanta, Georgia? Don't they realize a folksy, but deadly cross-examiner is on the case and ready to bring them to justice? *Matlock*, a legal TV drama series from 1986–1995, stars the legendary and lovable Andy Griffith as Atlanta attorney Benjamin Layton "Ben" Matlock. A widower, Matlock specializes in taking the tough murder cases no one else will touch. While Matlock may come across to his opponents as a slothful, laidback slacker, he's anything but.

DEADLY DIALOGUE

Ben Matlock: *Well. . . . There goes the killer.* —ANDY GRIFFITH AS BEN MATLOCK IN *MATLOCK* (1986–1995)

North Meets South in *Matlock*

Educated at Harvard Law School, Matlock integrates the best of the North with the best of the South. His knowledge of law, combined with his clever, Southern-sneak-up-on-'em style, leaves his legal opponents in a wake of legal confusion. The show's format is *Perry-Mason*esque, with Matlock defending an innocent client accused of murder and then ultimately exposing the true culprit in open court. Matlock's quirks give the show some delightful humor and the folksy charm of yesteryear.

The $100,000 Retainer

He can be hardheaded with his team of helpers, working them to the bone; is a glutton for hot dogs; and is overly thrifty even though he charges a $100,000 retainer. Matlock can always be found wearing the same wrinkled, gray/white suit everywhere he goes. Maybe law wasn't the only thing Matlock learned at Harvard. Perhaps the old, sly dog picked up a thing or two about Yankee thrift.

Don't Blame Sloth, Just Hell-Bent on Fishin'

Do people really hate all lawyers? If they do it's because they've never read William G. Tapply, creator of Boston attorney Brady Coyne. Tapply introduced readers to Coyne, a Vietnam veteran and fishing enthusiast, in 1984 with *Death at Charity's Point*. Brady hangs his shingle in cozy Copley Square, smack in the middle of Proper Boston. His elite clientele, however, are anything but proper (even when they pretend to be).

> *"Simply put, William G. Tapply is the best there is today at series fiction in this genre. A worthy successor to Hammett and both MacDonalds (Ross and John)."* —THE CHICAGO TRIBUNE

Fishing for Murder

Poor Brady just wants to scrape together enough money from his one-horse law practice to enjoy his true passion: fishing. Unfortunately, his Boston Brahmin clients always seem to end up facing a murder wrap and Brady finds himself solving one murder after another, often at great risk to himself.

The canon is not packed with courtroom drama and legal twists, but more the day-to-day grind of what it's really like to run a small law practice and face the dark side of the human condition.

Reading with the Fishes

In addition to *Charity's Point*, Brady would go on to appear in:

- *The Dutch Blue Error* (1985)
- *Follow the Sharks* (1985)
- *The Marine Corpse* (1986)
- *Dead Meat* (1987)
- *The Vulgar Boatman* (1987)
- *A Void of Hearts* (1988)
- *Dead Winter* (1989)
- *Client Privilege* (1989)
- *The Spotted Cats* (1991)
- *Tight Lines* (1992)
- *The Snake Eater* (1993)
- *The Seventh Enemy* (1995)
- *Close to the Bone* (1996)
- *Cutter's Run* (1998)
- *Muscle Memory* (1999)
- *Scar Tissue* (2000)
- *Past Tense* (2001)
- *A Fine Line* (2002)
- *Shadow of Death* (2003)
- *Nervous Water* (2005)
- *Out Cold* (2006)
- *One Way Ticket* (2007)
- *Hell Bent* (2008)
- *Outwitting Trolls* (2010)

The Quotable P.I. ——————————————————

V.I. Warshawski: *When in doubt, hesitate!* —KATHLEEN TURNER AS
V.I. WARSHAWSKI IN *V.I. WARSHAWSKI* (1991)

The Crime Lab from Hell

In February 2011, New York officials shut down their crime lab because,
they said, police knew that examiners were producing inaccurate measure-
ments in drug cases even before a national accrediting agency placed the lab
on probation.

Nearly 9,000 drug cases dating to late 2007 are currently being reviewed
for signs of errors after a spot check of nine cases involving ketamine or
ecstasy revealed that six of them were inaccurately analyzed.

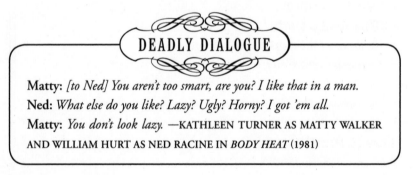

DEADLY DIALOGUE

Matty: *[to Ned] You aren't too smart, are you? I like that in a man.*
Ned: *What else do you like? Lazy? Ugly? Horny? I got 'em all.*
Matty: *You don't look lazy.* —KATHLEEN TURNER AS MATTY WALKER
AND WILLIAM HURT AS NED RACINE IN *BODY HEAT* (1981)

Forensic Failures

After discovering the massive lapses in protocol, officials immediately closed
the drug section of the crime lab. Nassau County District Attorney Kathleen Rice and County Executive Edward Mangano said new revelations that
police supervisors were aware of problems with ecstasy testing as far back as
September 2010, prompted the closure of the entire lab.

Detective Michael Bitsko, a police department spokesman, said county police are conducting an internal investigation "of the forensic evidence bureau, including the potential of supervisory awareness related to the testing inaccuracies."

X (Sort of) Marks the Spot

- Murder on Ecstasy, an experimental indie band from northern Virginia (last MySpace sign-on in 2009)
- *Death in Ecstasy*, a detective novel written by Ngaio Marsh in 1936, in which a woman is poisoned during a religious trance
- *Carnival Ecstasy*, a cruise ship that caught fire in 1998 en route to Key West (there were no fatalities) and spent six months as a floating hospital after Hurricane Katrina

The Quotable P.I.

Remington Steele: *Irresponsibility isn't a sickness—it's an art.* —PIERCE BROSNAN AS REMINGTON STEELE IN *REMINGTON STEELE* (1982–1987)

This Is Your Workplace on Drugs

Problems in Nassau first surfaced in December 2010, when a national accrediting group placed the lab on probation—the only lab in the country facing that sanction. The American Society of Crime Laboratory Directors/Laboratory Accreditation Board cited fifteen failures of the lab to comply with nationally recognized standards, including improper maintenance of equipment and instruments, failure to properly mark evidence, failure to properly store evidence, failure to secure the lab, and inadequate record-keeping.

Someone should contact Horatio Caine in Miami and tell him to come up to New York to check this out (sunglasses not needed).

> *"It's true hard work never killed anybody, but I figure, why take the chance?"* —RONALD REAGAN

First Lines

"The old lady had changed her mind about dying but by then it was too late." —*CITY OF BONES* (2002) BY MICHAEL CONNELLY

The Naked and the Dead Scientologist

Lisa McPherson, a member of the Church of Scientology, worked in Clearwater, Florida. Noting mental instability in her, the church had her undergo a process called Introspection Rundown. Later, she was in a minor auto accident. Though apparently unharmed, she began to disrobe. She was taken to a hospital but refused psychiatric examination, explaining she wanted to be helped by church members. She checked herself out and was taken by church members to Flag Land Base. Kept there for seventeen days, she became more and more incoherent, refusing food and deteriorating rapidly. She was finally taken to a hospital where, after efforts at resuscitation failed, she was declared dead.

In her initial death certificate, medical examiner Joan Wood said the blood clot that caused McPherson's death was due to "bed rest and severe dehydration." She listed the manner of death as "undetermined."

Best Two Out of Three

Which of the following felony criminal charges did the Clearwater branch of the Church of Scientology face because Lisa McPherson had been in their care for more than two weeks before her death?

1. Abuse of a disabled adult
2. Second degree felony murder
3. Practicing medicine without a license

ANSWERS: 1 and 3

The Waffling Joan Wood

The church hired two forensic pathologists who disputed medical examiner Joan Wood's findings about McPherson's death.

Wood changed her conclusion to read the death was an "accident" not caused by dehydration. She then changed it again, reinserting "dehydration" as a cause of death and listing the death as a homicide. The next morning, she changed her mind once again and finalized the changes.

Eventually, the state of Florida was forced to drop criminal charges against the Church of Scientology based, to a considerable degree, on Dr. Wood's failure to make up her mind. Dr. Wood was forced to retire after spending eighteen years as the medical examiner for Pinellas and Pasco counties because she made a mess of the case against the Church of Scientology. But that wasn't Wood's only mistake.

An M.E.'s Misjudgment

While the Church of Scientology may have escaped prosecution because of Dr. Wood, David Long spent forty-nine days in jail wrongly convicted of his child's death because of her testimony.

The Longs' Sad Story

Rebecca Long was the Longs' prematurely born infant daughter with serious health problems. Rebecca had been crying and, when she stopped, David looked in to check on her. He found her facedown and not breathing so she was rushed to a hospital, but it was too late.

The next day David was told he was a suspect in the baby's death. Dr. Wood had determined that Rebecca had died of shaken-baby syndrome. Based on Wood's testimony, a grand jury later indicted him on first-degree murder charges.

Get Second Opinions

Detective Jeff Bousquet, who investigated the case, never felt Long was guilty. At Bousquet's request, Jon Thogmartin, who replaced Wood as medical examiner, looked into the case.

Wood's autopsy report was plagued with problems. There were discrepancies with the medical findings and not a shred of evidence to prove Baby Rebecca was even abused.

"Rebecca Long did not have trauma," Thogmartin said.

In Joan Wood's report, she wrote the brain has "no distinct areas of hemorrhage," but in the next paragraph she contradicts that statement, claiming, "the brain has . . . hemorrhage."

The report goes on to state Rebecca had retinal hemorrhaging—bleeding in the eyes—which is caused when a baby is shaken. However, Thogmartin and four other pathologists found there was no evidence of that.

Wood also listed Rebecca as a baby boy.

Wrongly Accused

Though he was released from prison, David Long had the stigma of having been charged with murder. He lost his job and all his assets in bankruptcy. Not to mention his Baby Rebecca.

Want to Be Really Lazy? Be Your Own Boss

Q: What other position did Joan Wood hold while she served as the medical examiner for Pinellas and Pasco counties?

A: Dr. Wood was simultaneously the chairperson of Florida's Medical Examiner's Commission, the commission that regulates medical examiners. In other words, she was her own supervisor.

Locard's Exchange Principle

> *"It is impossible for a criminal to act, especially considering the intensity of a crime, without leaving traces of his presence."* —EDMUND LOCARD

There's No Such Thing as the Perfect Crime

Edmund Locard (1877–1966), a French forensic scientist, was the director of the first crime laboratory (Lyon, France, 1910). He began it in an attic with two assistants. In the early twentieth century, he postulated his famous Locard's Exchange Principle—the heart of forensics.

Simply put, he hypothesized that if someone makes contact with another person, place, or thing, there is some exchange between the two. Everyone leaves something in their wake.

Screwing Up the Scene of the Crime

Justice is rarely served when investigators are too careless and mishandle the traces clearly left behind from a crime. Take the case of Kevin Hoffman, for instance. He was accused as an accomplice to the murder of Michael Sortal in Broward County, Florida, in 2001. According to Locard's principle, he should have left something behind. He did. His DNA was found at the scene along with that of Geoffrey Kennedy, who was found guilty and sentenced to life. Hoffman's attorney claimed there had been a mistake made with Hoffman's DNA testing and asked that it be tested again. During the retest, however, Hoffman's DNA was accidently mixed with the DNA from a separate case. They couldn't save the DNA and without it, the charges were dropped. Hoffman, however, was still being charged with a home invasion and attempted murder that had been committed two weeks before Sortal was killed. He was sentenced to two years house arrest and thirty years probation on that crime.

When Clothing Speaks Louder than Words

Two golfers are in a locker room. One asks his buddy, "Hey, how long have you been wearing a girdle?" His friend answers, "Ever since my wife found it in our car."

> *"The kindest word to describe my performance in school was Sloth."*
> —HARRISON FORD

In the Clear—Not!

A little over a month later, Hoffman was recharged with Sortal's murder. Detectives were able to submit different evidence from the crime scene. Six inmates came forward and stated that while in prison Hoffman had implicated himself in the murder. And Hoffman's codefendant, Kennedy, had finally agreed to testify against Hoffman. This time the crime scene evidence was submitted to the Florida Department of Law Enforcement Lab and not the Broward lab where the first sample of DNA had been contaminated.

BLOOD & BONES

"It will never be possible to eliminate all chance of error or misjudgment, but the Forensic Science Service strives to do the greatest good for the greatest number, for the greatest part of time." —PROFESSOR MICHAEL GREEN, UNIVERSITY OF SHEFFIELD

WRATH

n., from the Old English *wraththu*, meaning angry

1. Anger; rage
2. Punishment; vengeance
3. Divine retribution
4. A fit of temper

"In the souls of the people the grapes of wrath are filling and growing heavy, growing heavy for the vintage." —JOHN STEINBECK

The worst crimes against humanity are committed in the name of wrath. Sometimes this profound anger against one's fellow and sister humans is stoked first in the fires of religion, but it is also stoked in the fires of the twisted psyches of murderers, rapists, and serial killers. Many of these crimes are unspeakable—and yet they speak to the darkness inside us all.

> *"Indulge not thyself in the passion of anger; it is whetting a sword to wound thine own breast, or murder thy friend."* —AKHENATON, PHARAOH OF THE EIGHTEENTH EGYPTIAN DYNASTY

Twelve Angry White Men = Jury from Hell

Have you ever had to place your life in the hands of a handful of strangers? Angry strangers? What goes on while a jury deliberates has long been a mystery even to those closest to the criminal justice system.

There is perhaps no better study of this mystery than Reginald Rose's play *Twelve Angry Men* (1954). The play is structured around the whims, personal interests, prejudices, and examples of human frailty and ultimately how one man with courage can make a difference. The conflict of the play is simple, yet its resolution is complex and full of tension. Twelve white men are trapped in a jury room and cannot leave until they have decided the fate of an African American defendant charged with murder, a rap based on circumstantial evidence.

⊗ First Lines

"Judge: Murder in the first degree—premeditated homicide—is the most serious charge tried in our criminal courts. You've heard a long and complex case, gentlemen, and it is now your duty to sit down to try and separate the facts from the fancy. One man is dead. The life of another is at stake. If there is a reasonable doubt in your minds as to the guilt of the accused . . . then you must declare him not guilty. If, however, there is no reasonable doubt, then he must be found guilty. Whichever way you decide, the verdict must be unanimous. I urge you to deliberate honestly and thoughtfully. You are faced with a grave responsibility. Thank you, gentlemen." —*TWELVE ANGRY MEN* (1954) BY REGINALD ROSE

Vote for the Status Quo

On the first vote, before the evidence is even analyzed, all the jurors vote to convict with the exception of one dissenter. For some jurors the basis for conviction is primarily that the defendant is African American. For others it is sloth, ignorance, and the fear of not siding with the majority.

COP TALK: MACHISMO SPEAKS!

Hans Gruber: *Who are you then?*
John McClane: *Just a fly in the ointment, Hans. The monkey in the wrench.*
—BRUCE WILLIS AS DETECTIVE JOHN MCCLANE AND ALAN RICKMAN
AS HANS GRUBER IN *DIE HARD* (1988)

DEADLY DIALOGUE

Juror #3: *Brother, I've seen all kinds of dishonesty in my day, but this little display takes the cake. Y'all come in here with your hearts bleedin' all over the floor about slum kids and injustice; you listen to some fairy tales; suddenly you start getting through to some of these old ladies . . . well, you're not getting through to me, I've had enough! What's the matter with you guys? You all know he's guilty. He's got to burn! You're letting him slip through our fingers.* —LEE J. COBB AS JUROR #3 IN *12 ANGRY MEN* (1957)

"For every minute you remain angry, you give up sixty seconds of peace of mind." —RALPH WALDO EMERSON

Vote for the Constitution

The fate of the defendant rests with man's whims and weaknesses and the path of least resistance. The time is 1957, long before civil rights, and the place is a smoke-filled juror room in the Halls of Justice. The one holdout, played by Henry Fonda in the 1957 film version, is intent on doing the job he has been charged with by the Constitution—drafted by white men. He ironically becomes a minority and, in many ways, a traitor to his "people" for wanting to give the defendant a fair shake.

Twelve Angry Men Make a Movie—Twice!

Q: Name the two Academy-Award–winning actors who starred in the movie version of *12 Angry Men*.

A: The play that so expertly dissects human nature and all its weaknesses and strengths was made into a film twice: once in 1957 starring Henry Fonda and again in 1997 starring Jack Lemmon.

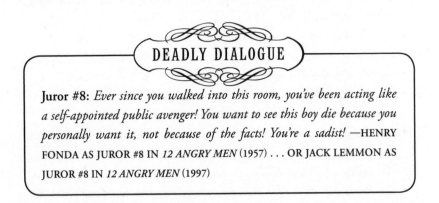

DEADLY DIALOGUE

Juror #8: *Ever since you walked into this room, you've been acting like a self-appointed public avenger! You want to see this boy die because you personally want it, not because of the facts! You're a sadist!* —HENRY FONDA AS JUROR #8 IN *12 ANGRY MEN* (1957) . . . OR JACK LEMMON AS JUROR #8 IN *12 ANGRY MEN* (1997)

The Battle of the Murdering Sexes

Men are ten times more likely than women to be murderers and fourteen times more likely to kill more than once.

Ten Movies about Real Serial Killers

- *The Deliberate Stranger* (1986). Mark Harmon plays Ted Bundy, the man responsible for the deaths of at least thirty women from Washington State to Florida over the course of more than a decade.
- *To Catch a Killer* (1992). Brian Dennehy plays John Wayne Gacy, a homicidal monster who tortured and murdered more than two dozen young victims and buried them in the crawlspace beneath his house.
- *Zodiac* (2007). Jake Gyllenhaal plays a *San Fancisco Chronicle* cartoonist taunted with letters and ciphers from a Bay-area serial killer who was never caught.
- *Dahmer* (2002). David Jacobson wrote and directed this movie about Jeffrey Dahmer, who killed fifteen boys and cannibalized their remains.
- *Ed Gein* (2000). Steve Railsback stars as Ed Gein, a 1950s Wisconsin farmer who was a deeply disturbed serial killer. The Gein case inspired movies like *Psycho*.
- *The Boston Strangler* (1968). Tony Curtis plays Albert DeSalvo, who confessed to a rape and killing spree of thirteen women in the early 1960s in Boston.
- *The Case of the Hillside Stranglers* (TV 1989). Dennis Farina and Billy Zane play two cousins responsible for a series of murders in the hills above Los Angeles.
- *Henry: Portrait of a Serial Killer* (1986). This movie is loosely based on the case of Henry Lee Lucas, a confessed serial killer.
- *Summer of Sam* (1999). Spike Lee crafted this portrayal of the Bronx in the summer of 1977 when the Son of Sam (David Berkowitz) terrorized the city by stalking and killing lovers parked in vehicles on dark streets.
- *The Riverman* (TV 2004). Based on interviews with convicted serial killer Ted Bundy (Cary Elwes), conducted by investigators hunting a serial killer in Seattle, later identified as Gary Ridgway.

KILLER WIT

"Always make the audience suffer as much as possible."
—ALFRED HITCHCOCK

Are You Feeling Lucky?

Name the Dirty Harry movie:

Harry Callahan: You know, you're crazy if you think you've heard the last of this guy. He's gonna kill again.
District Attorney Rothko: How do you know?
Harry Callahan: 'Cause he likes it.

ANSWER: *Dirty Harry* (1971)

But Don't Count the Women Out

Men may be more violent than women, overall, but the bad girls' stats are nonetheless impressive (and not in a good way). Women commit:

- 30 percent of murders within a family
- 34 percent of intimate-partner killings
- 48 percent of infanticides
- 15 percent of murders of the elderly

DEADLY DIALOGUE

Lisbeth Salander: *"I've never done this before. Hold still, or it'll get messy."*—LISBETH SALANDER IN *THE GIRL WITH THE DRAGON TATTOO* (2004) BY STIEG LARSSON

(Almost) First Lines

"One of the myths that has been perpetuated by the press and popular media is that serial murders are invariably and exclusively committed by men." —*MURDER MOST RARE: THE FEMALE SERIAL KILLER* (1998) BY MICHAEL D. KELLEHER AND C. L. KELLEHER

Next Time Won't You Slay with Me?

Q: Which Agatha Christie novel features a serial killer?

A: In 1936, Christie wrote her seventeenth novel, *The ABC Murders*. The story features her famous protagonist Hercule Poirot, who must use his "little gray cells" to solve a maddening string of alphabetically linked murders.

"In fact, the genuine history of this crime is replete with dozens of female serial killers who were far more lethal—and often far more successful in their determination to kill—than their male counterparts. . . . The female serial killer typically remains undetected for a significantly longer period of time than the average male serial murderer. She is a quiet killer, who is often painstakingly methodical and eminently lethal in her actions." —"INTRODUCTION," *MURDER MOST RARE: THE FEMALE SERIAL KILLER*

The Smartest Serial Killers Are Women

On average, female serial killers in the United States are active for more than ten years before being caught, twice as long as males. (Source: Bureau of Justice Statistics, *Homicide Type by Gender, 1976–2005*)

A Femme Fatale by Any Other Name

Infamous female killers earn their share of nicknames as well. Match these murdering women by their colorful aliases:

1. The Bloody Countess	a. Marie Besnard
2. Duchess of Death	b. Elizabeth Blathory
3. The Giggling Granny	c. Louise Peete
4. Queen of Poisoners	d. Belle Gunness
5. Lady Rotten	e. Mary Ann Cotton
6. Lady Bluebeard/Hell's Belle	f. Nannie Doss

ANSWERS: 1-b; 2-c; 3-f; 4-a; 5-e; 6-d

Wicked Witch of the Middle East

Q: Which mystery writer inspired Iran's first female serial killer?

A: Iranian police claim a woman named Mahin confessed to killing at least six people, including five women, using methods described in Agatha Christie novels to evade detection. Iranian law enforcement arrested the accused serial killer in the city of Qazvin in May 2009.

"Anger and jealousy can no more bear to lose sight of their objects than love." —GEORGE ELIOT

Killer Facts

Thirty-two-year-old Mahin allegedly approached each of the elderly women after prayers, and offered them rides home, a gesture she attributed to their reminding her of her own mother. But instead of taking them home, she gave them fruit juice laced with knock-out drugs, pocketed their cash and jewelry, and then strangled them and dumped their bodies. Authorities claim that her motive was twofold: 1) pay off $25,000 in debt, and 2) act out her "intense hatred toward her mother."

> *"A curious thing about atrocity stories is that they mirror, instead of the events they purport to describe, the extent of the hatred of the people that tell them. Still, you can't listen unmoved to tales of misery and murder."*
> —JOHN DOS PASSOS

A Page Out of Agatha's Book

If Mahin's story sounds like something out of an Agatha Christie novel, maybe that's because it is. Mahin allegedly drew her inspiration from the bestselling mysteries, which are very popular in Iran (and not just among serial killers). Christie traveled to Iran on more than one occasion, and even set one of her stories—"The House at Shiraz"—in Iran.

> *"The why of murder always fascinates me so much more than the how."*
> —ANN RULE

Ann Rules!

True crime writer Ann Rule has published two dozen books and more than 1,400 articles, most of them on real criminal cases. Born into a family of law enforcers, she is herself a former Seattle police officer, public assistance caseworker, and student intern at an Oregon training school for girls. She has a BA from the University of Washington in Creative Writing, with minors in psychology, criminology, and penology and she continues to take college credit courses on topics in criminology, forensics, and law enforcement. Rule was selected for the task force that set up the Violent Criminal Apprehension Program (VI-CAP) and has testified before Congress on victims' rights and the danger of serial killers.

And Now for the Next Serial Killer

Bestselling author Ann Rule has specialized in documenting the most gruesome murders of our time. Match the books to the alleged killers in this mini-bibliography:

1. *The Stranger Beside Me* (1980)

2. *Too Late to Say Goodbye* (2007)

3. *Green River, Running Red* (2004)

4. *Dead by Sunset* (1995)

5. *Heart Full of Lies* (2003)

6. *In the Still of the Night* (2010)

a. Bart Corbin

b. Liysa Northon

c. Ted Bundy

d. Gary Leon Ridgway

e. Brad Cunningham

f. Ron Reynolds

ANSWERS: 1-c; 2-a; 3-d; 4-e; 5-b; 6-f

Too Close for Comfort

Q: What serial killer did true crime writer Ann Rule know personally?

A: Ted Bundy, the subject of *The Stranger Beside Me*, began working with Ann Rule at Seattle's Suicide Hot Line Crisis Center in 1971.

If You Like Slasher Films, You Could Be a Serial Killer...

After his capture and conviction, serial killer Ted Bundy proposed this plan for catching the competition, the Green River Killer in Washington State: "Years ago I read about a psychiatrist who said, 'If you could only photograph everybody who came out of *The Texas Chainsaw Massacre*, you would have a mug book of all the active violent offenders against women in that particular area.' And I would have to say that he was right on the mark. . . . Have a slasher film festival! . . . It'd be like, you know, bees to honey."

> "Hatchet murders were the house speciality of the [New York] Journal, whose front page was a virtual abattoir of murder most foul." —LEE ISRAEL

A Real Texas Chainsaw Massacre

The stuff of slasher movies and nightmares, the chainsaw—no, two chainsaws—were used to decapitate and dismember a woman in Lewisville, Texas. On April 26, 2010, police found two bloody chainsaws at the scene of a gruesome murder.

Detectives say forty-nine-year-old Jose Fernando Corona decapitated and dismembered his forty-four-year-old wife, Maria, and left her body in the street in front of their home on Shadow Wood Drive.

Call Your Dead Mother, Please

According to police, a mail carrier discovered Maria's mutilated body around 11:20 A.M., and saw a trail of blood and hair leading into the house.

Moments after police arrived on the scene, one of the Coronas' six children arrived with her husband. Carla Corona said her father had telephoned her moments before, saying that he had finally done it, that he had finally killed his wife and that he was going to drag the body next door.

Carla tried in vain to call her mother but didn't get an answer. She and her husband identified her mother's remains on the street.

Police found two chainsaws on the open bed of Jose Corona's white pickup work truck, both stained with blood. One of them was still running.

Still Running, Act II

Corona is still on the run and wanted on a charge of murder. Police say he may be driving a gold 1991 Ford Ranger pickup.

"Anybody who's been through a divorce will tell you that at one point . . . they've thought murder. The line between thinking murder and doing murder isn't that major." —OLIVER STONE

KILLER WIT

"To simply scare the hell out of people."

—ALFRED HITCHCOCK, ON HIS MISSION IN LIFE

Alias "Scumbag"

The popular news media loves to give killers fanciful nicknames—a practice law enforcement discourages. Some killers seem to feel unloved if they don't get a fancy moniker and even suggest their own. How many of these aliases do you recognize?

1. The Boston Strangler

2. The BTK Strangler

3. The Clown Killer

4. The .44 Caliber Killer/Son of Sam

5. The Green River Killer

6. The Campus Killer/Lady Killer

7. The Machete Murderer

8. The Milwaukee Monster

9. The Pied Piper of Tucson

10. The Yorkshire Ripper

a. David Berkowitz

b. Charles Schmid

c. Theodore Bundy

d. Albert DeSalvo

e. John Wayne Gacy

f. Juan Corona

g. Peter Sutcliffe

h. Dennis Rader

i. Jeffrey Dahmer

j. Gary Leon Ridgway

ANSWERS: 1-d; 2-h; 3-e; 4-a; 5-j; 6-c; 7-f; 8-i; 9-b; 10-g

What's with the Name?

Victims have won popular nicknames, too. Elizabeth Short's posthumous epithet "The Black Dahlia" seems to be a play on *The Blue Dahlia*, a 1946 film noir starring Alan Ladd and Veronica Lake. In it, a woman is murdered after living a reckless life—a story not unlike Short's, who was found tortured and brutalized in 1947. The Black Dahlia case is still unsolved.

Stranger Than Fiction

Q: What other real-life murder caused novelist James Ellroy's fascination with the Black Dahlia case?

A: Ellroy's mother was found strangled in 1958, her body dumped in bushes near an athletic field. Ten-year-old Ellroy was spending a summer weekend with his father, so Jean Ellroy had gone out to a bar the night before. Ellroy said he channeled his emotions into an interest in the 1947 torture-murder of Elizabeth Short, a young woman who shared some of the wild characteristics and risky behavior of his mother.

Looking for Answers in Fact and Fiction

Before Ellroy wrote *The Black Dahlia* (1987), his novel about that case, he wrote a fictionalized account of his mother's murder, *Clandestine* (1982). In 1994, he enlisted the help of an investigator to try to find her killer, but too many suspects had died. Both cases remain unsolved.

COP TALK: MACHISMO SPEAKS!

Roger Murtaugh: *God hates me. That's what it is.*

Martin Riggs: *Hate him back; it works for me.*

—MEL GIBSON AS SERGEANT MARTIN RIGGS AND DANNY GLOVER AS DETECTIVE ROGER MURTAUGH IN *LETHAL WEAPON* (1987)

War Games

"To the sociologist, she is the typical, unfortunate depression child who matured too suddenly in her teens into the easy money, easy living, easy loving of wartime America." —"THE BLACK DAHLIA" IN *THE BADGE* (1958) BY JACK WEBB

∾ First Lines

"The road to the partnership began without my knowing it, and it was a revival of the Blanchard-Bleichert fight brouhaha that brought me the word." —*THE BLACK DAHLIA* (1987) **BY JAMES ELLROY**

Sounds Like Murder to Me

- A shrewdness of apes
- A troop of baboons
- A sleuth of bears
- A clash of bucks
- An army of caterpillars
- An intrusion of cockroaches
- A band of coyotes
- A murder of crows
- A gang of elk
- A skulk of foxes
- An army of frogs
- A horde of gnats
- A troubling of goldfish
- A pack of grouse
- A brood of hens
- A mob of kangaroo
- A desert of lapwings
- A plague of locusts
- A gulp of magpies
- A mischief of mice
- An unkindness of ravens
- An ambush of tigers
- A pitying of turtledoves
- A nest of vipers
- A fall of woodcock

KILLER WIT

"Seeing a murder on television can help work off one's antagonisms. And if you haven't any antagonisms, the commercials will give you some."
—ALFRED HITCHCOCK

Bible Bedtime Stories: Hung by a Hair

While technically a battlefield casualty, Absalom's killing was unnecessary. During a battle against the forces of his father, King David, Absalom, riding a mule, got his long hair caught in the branches of an oak tree. The mule ran on, leaving Absalom hanging. Joab, David's field commander, heard about it, hurried to the tree, and thrust a spear into Absalom. Joab's guards finished Absalom off. David's response to the sight left William Faulkner with a good book title.

"If you murder an innocent man you are responsible for the blood of his unborn descendants, and the weight of this responsibility is yours to carry to the end of time." —UNKNOWN

The Quotable P.I. ―――――――――――――――――――――

"I don't mind if you don't like my manners, I don't like them myself. They are pretty bad. I grieve over them on long winter evenings."
—HUMPHREY BOGART AS P.I. PHILIP MARLOWE IN *THE BIG SLEEP* (1946)

Kill Him Dead, Dead, Dead!

Conspirators determined to assassinate Grigori Rasputin knew he'd be a hard man to kill. A marked man thanks to his influence over the Russian imperial family, the so-called Mad Monk had long been the target of assassination attempts:

- Attempt #1: Disembowelment. Rasputin was disemboweled by a single attacker in 1914—and survived.
- Attempt #2: Poisoning. According to legend, assassins poisoned Rasputin in December 1916 with five times the lethal dose of cyanide.
- Attempt #3: Beating and Shooting. When the killers came to dispose of the body, Rasputin tried to strangle one of the attackers. They then shot him four times and clubbed him into unconsciousness.
- Attempt #4: Drowning. Not taking any chances, the assassins then wrapped Rasputin's body in a rug and threw it into the icy Neva River.

> *"When the bell tolls three times, it will announce that I have been killed. If I am killed by common men, you and your children will rule Russia for centuries to come; if I am killed by one of your stock, you and your family will be killed by the Russian people! Pray, Tsar of Russia. Pray."*
> —RASPUTIN

BLOOD & BONES

"It is always hazardous to conclude that a person could not have done some rational act after receiving gunshot wounds in vital organs."
—LEMOYNE SNYDER

Rasputin Rises Again

After the fourth assassination attempt, when the body was discovered three days later, legend claims Rasputin's arms were free of the bindings and an autopsy determined the cause of death was drowning. Several months later, after the February Revolution, workers dug up his body to be burned. To their horror, Rasputin seemed to sit up and move!—an effect created by the shrinking of the tendons.

Leave It to the Spies

More recent evidence indicates Rasputin was probably not poisoned or drowned, but was beaten, attacked with a bladed weapon, and shot. The most intriguing claim is that Rasputin was targeted by Britain's Secret Intelligence Service (later MI6), and the fatal shot through the forehead came from a Webley revolver used by the SIS. (Source: *Six: A History of Britain's Secret Intelligence Service* [2010] by Michael Smith)

> ### COP TALK: MAD AS HELL
> **Harry Callahan:** *Nothing wrong with shooting as long as the right people get shot!*
> —CLINT EASTWOOD AS INSPECTOR "DIRTY" HARRY CALLAHAN IN *MAGNUM FORCE* (1973)

> ### COP TALK: MACHISMO SPEAKS!
> **Abel Turner:** *I am the police! You *have* to do what I say!*
> —SAMUEL L. JACKSON AS LAPD OFFICER ABEL TURNER IN *LAKEVIEW TERRACE* (2008)

When Cops See Red
- *Acts of Vengeance* (2003) by Frank Smith
- *The Angel Maker* (1993) by Ridley Pearson
- *Cop Hater* (1956) by Ed McBain
- *Crossing the Line* (2004) by Clinton McKinzie
- *Final Justice* (2003) by W. E. B. Griffin
- *Gideon's Wrath* (1967) by J. J. Marric
- "Mean Streak" (1988) by Philip Cordwainer
- *Road Rage* (1997) by Ruth Rendell
- *A Suitable Vengeance* (1991) by Elizabeth George
- *Vengeance in Death* (1997) by J. D. Robb

Cool, Calm, and Collected

One of the major reasons someone hires a private investigator is that that person is objective. Being objective, the P.I. is not distracted by high emotions that would interfere with solving the case, not unless the guilty party makes the mistake of going after the P.I. Do that, and objectivity is thrown out the window. Then, it's personal.

Hell Hath No Fury Like a P.I.

After being left shackled in a remote cabin to die, the Nameless Detective focuses his hate and rage to survive, escape, and then find his adversary. (*Shackles* [1988] by Bill Pronzini)

A Riot of Cops

While movie police of the thirties, forties, and fifties were happy enough to do their jobs, that changed in the late sixties and seventies as the public grew weary of injustice. Steve McQueen as Lieutenant Frank Bullitt (Bullitt, 1968) and Clint Eastwood as Inspector "Dirty" Harry Callahan

(*Dirty Harry*, 1971) simmered with rage at how the system kept them from doing their jobs.

ᔓ *First Lines*

"*In death there was no love in his face. Or kindness. Or peace. There had been little of any of these in life either but I had not known him then and would not learn that until later.*" —*KAT SCRATCH FEVER* (1997) BY KAREN KIJEWSKI

Hell Hath No Fury Like a P.I.—and Pal

After his friend Hawk is brutally attacked and left for dead, Spenser joins Hawk in a bloody trail of revenge. (*Cold Service* [2005] by Robert B. Parker)

Not with Our Sister, You Don't

The sons of Jacob were not known for moderation or restraint in the best of circumstances, so when their sister Dinah was raped (or at least disgraced) by a Canaanite prince, they reacted violently (see Genesis 34). Dinah had attracted the attention of Shechem, son of the Hivite ruler, Hamor. According to various sources, he persuaded her to submit to him, raped her outright, or carried her off in the tradition of abduction marriage. In any case, "his heart was drawn to Dinah," and Shechem and Hamor offered Jacob any bride-price to agree to a marriage.

Jacob's sons pretended to accept the proposal and other intermarriages if all the Hivite men would agree to be circumcised. Lured by the prospect of generous bride-prices, the Hivite men all went under the knife. But the brothers' anger with the Hivites was far from quelled.

> *"Three days later, while all of them were still in pain, two of Jacob's sons, Simeon and Levi, Dinah's brothers, took their swords and attacked the unsuspecting city, killing every male."* —GENESIS 34:25 NIV

Getting Mad, and Getting Even

Not to be left out, Jacob's other sons looted the city, carrying off all the cattle, household goods, and women and children. As a punishment for slaying innocent men, Jacob refused Simeon and Levi an equal share of the land of Israel.

The Bible Brothers from Hell

In the Bible, no one ever bothered to tell Dinah's side of the story. It was all about the boys—until Anita Diamant wrote her bestselling novel. In *The Red Tent* Diamant tells the story from Dinah's point of view. Suffice it to say that Dinah was not pleased with her brothers.

> *"Revenge is barren of itself: it is the dreadful food it feeds on; its delight is murder, and its end is despair."* —FRIEDRICH SCHILLER

ᘒ *First Lines*

"In the ninth book of The Republic, *Plato famously observed that 'the virtuous man is content to dream what a wicked man really does.'"*
—*TRUE CRIME: AN AMERICAN ANTHOLOGY* (2008) EDITED BY HAROLD SCHECHTER

The Infamous Code of Silence

According to the DEA, from 1975 through 1992 Charlestown, Massachusetts, experienced some forty-nine murders and thirty-three of them remain unsolved because witnesses feared retaliation if they cooperated with the cops. Most of Charlestown's murders can be traced to drugs, armored car robberies, and informants who dared to ignore the notorious code of silence. When it comes to this one square mile of Boston, greed knows no boundaries.

Under Oath of Silence

In her breakout legal suspense novel *Under Oath*, former nuts-and-bolts prosecutor Margaret McLean takes a hard, inside look at the infamous Charlestown "Code of Silence."

In some of the best and most authentic courtroom scenes in any novel, *Under Oath* conducts a thorough examination of the Charlestown streets, culture, and undisputed title as America's unsolved murder capital.

COP TALK: MAD AS HELL

Harry Callahan: *I don't like your list, Swan. I don't like being on it.*

Peter Swan: *Ah, that's, that's what this is really all about, isn't it? Well, if you got a charge to make. . .*

Harry Callahan: *Maybe I'll start my own dead pool, and put you on it.*

Peter Swan: *You threatening me?*

Harry Callahan: *You want to play the game, you'd better know the rules, love.*

—CLINT EASTWOOD AS INSPECTOR "DIRTY" HARRY CALLAHAN AND LIAM NEESON AS PETER SWAN IN *THE DEAD POOL* (1988)

Every Cop Knows

- You've got to keep your emotional distance if you're going to do the job.
- Some cases, some victims still get to you—and you've still got to do the job.

The Search for Justice

The disappearance of twenty-five-year-old Amy St. Laurent in October 2001 prompted a seven-week intensive search across southern Maine by the Portland police, several other town departments, the county sheriff's office, the Maine State Police, the marine patrol, the Coast Guard, the National Guard, the Maine Warden's Service, state search and rescue volunteers, and ordinary citizens.

Soon after Amy's disappearance during a night in downtown Portland with friends, police were certain she had been killed and almost certain they knew who did it: the man who claimed he'd dropped her off outside a club after a party at his apartment. As the weeks passed, the suspect's story began to unravel, but without a body, police still had no evidence of a crime. And the first snow would soon fall.

℘ First Lines

"It's every parent's nightmare—your child goes out one Saturday night and vanishes off the face of the earth." —FINDING AMY (2006) BY CAPTAIN JOSEPH K. LOUGHLIN AND KATE CLARK FLORA

Finding Amy

On December 8, more than 100 people and dog teams searched a wooded area identified as the most likely of nineteen possible "dump sites" linked to the suspect. More than six hours later, they found Amy's grave. Her murderer was tried and convicted.

> "We're supposed to box it up. Lock it out and get on with the job. I've stored up twenty-plus years of stifling my emotions while witnessing the howl of human agony. Now I worry it will come spilling out."
> —CAPTAIN JOSEPH K. LOUGHLIN

BLOOD & BONES

"As those who study them have come to learn, bones make good witnesses—although they speak softly, they never lie, and they never forget." —DR. CLYDE COLLINS SNOW, FORENSIC ANTHROPOLOGIST

Anger and the Avenging Writer

Q: What inspired John Grisham's first novel, *A Time to Kill* (1989), and hence led to a brilliant literary career in the legal crime fiction novel and beyond?

A: Righteous anger and wrath. After Grisham received his law degree from the University of Mississippi, he went on to practice criminal law for almost a decade. One day, as a spectator, he sat in on a criminal trial and watched a young girl bravely testify against the man who brutally raped her. As Grisham watched the proceedings, he thought about how difficult it must have been for this little girl and her family to have to relive the horrific events.

> "I watched her suffer before the jury, I wanted to personally shoot the rapist. For one brief yet interminable moment, I wanted to be her father. I wanted justice. There was a story there." —JOHN GRISHAM, ON THE TRIAL THAT INSPIRED *A TIME TO KILL* (1989)

COP TALK: MAD AS HELL

Harry Callahan: *I know what you're thinking. "Did he fire six shots or only five?" Well, to tell you the truth, in all this excitement I kind of lost track myself. But being as this is a .44 Magnum, the most powerful handgun in the world, and would blow your head clean off, you've got to ask yourself one question: Do I feel lucky? Well, do ya, punk?*

—CLINT EASTWOOD AS INSPECTOR "DIRTY" HARRY CALLAHAN IN *DIRTY HARRY* (1971)

"I love the idea of somebody freezing a body and then dancing with it; there's something rather sweet about it." —MARY HIGGINS CLARK, ON *LOVES MUSIC, LOVES TO DANCE* (1992)

Revenge Is Best Served Very Cold

Lawyer-writer Lisa Scottoline proves in her legal thriller *The Vendetta Defense* (2001) that elephants aren't the only animals that never forget. Protagonist Antonio Lucia is an Italian immigrant now living in Philly and has earned the moniker "Pigeon Tony" because he raises and trains pigeons.

Pigeon Tony is a seventy-nine-year-old man hell-bent on getting his pound of flesh from Angelo Coluzzi. Pigeon Tony believes Coluzzi is responsible for the death of his wife some half-century ago, and the passage of time has done nothing to diminish the grudge. As a result, when Pigeon Tony catches up with Coluzzi at a local pigeon club, he murders him.

The All-American Vigilante Hero

A troubled past void of justice makes Pigeon Tony a sympathetic killer or an avenger. Like the inverted mystery, Columbo-style, the hook of the story is not whether Pigeon committed the murder, but whether he will get sprung or spend his remaining days a jailbird.

The Quotable P.I.

"That rug really tied the room together." —JEFF BRIDGES AS JEFFREY "THE DUDE" LEBOWSKI IN *THE BIG LEBOWSKI* (1998)

Vigilante Heroes on the Screen

Match the actor to the film in which he or she plays an avenging angel:

1. *Law Abiding Citizen* (2009)
2. *Death Wish* (1974)
3. *Falling Down* (1993)
4. *Taken* (2008)
5. *Ransom* (1996)
6. *Gran Torino* (2008)
7. *The Brave One* (2007)
8. *The Godfather* (1972)

a. Jodie Foster
b. Liam Neeson
c. Michael Douglas
d. Al Pacino
e. Gerard Butler
f. Mel Gibson
g. Charles Bronson
h. Clint Eastwood

ANSWERS: 1-e; 2-g; 3-c; 4-b; 5-f; 6-h; 7-a; 8-d

Neighbors . . . Or Vigilantes?

Q: Who founded the Guardian Angels, the controversial crime-fighting organization with members in cities across America?

A: Curtis Sliwa founded the beret-wearing anti-crime group in 1979.

DEADLY DIALOGUE

Rooster: *A righteous man before me stands. A hero in these filthy lands. A brother in arms in heart are you. I was really hoping you get it too.*
—AL PACINO AS DETECTIVE ROOSTER IN *RIGHTEOUS KILL* (2008)

For the Love of Hate

Q: Who is the most beloved and respected lawyer in American literature?

A: Atticus Finch, the hero of Harper Lee's classic novel, *To Kill a Mockingbird* (1960). Finch, a Great Depression lawyer in the Deep South town of Maycomb, Alabama, embodies everything a lawyer ought to be. For him, justice, not the almighty dollar, is his motivating force in the courtroom. So when a local black man, Tom Robinson, is falsely accused of raping a white woman, Finch takes on the case, knowing that he himself will now become despised in the community, perhaps lose his law practice, and maybe even be killed for taking the word of a black man over a white woman—and probably never get paid.

Through the Eyes of a Child

In her 1960 Pulitzer Prize–winning novel, Lee tells the story through the eyes of Finch's young daughter, Scout, who observes her father's courage during his representation of Robinson and gets an early lesson on racial injustice. Not to mention the price one pays for having the courage to fight the evils born from pride, lust, and wrath.

> *"I wanted you to see what real courage is, instead of getting the idea that courage is a man with a gun in his hand. It's when you know you're licked before you begin but you begin anyway and you see it through no matter what. You rarely win, but sometimes you do."* —ATTICUS FINCH IN *TO KILL A MOCKINGBIRD* (1960) BY HARPER LEE

✑ *First Lines*

"Detective Superintendent Harriet Martens spat out her bottled rage. 'I'm going to resign from this bloody job.'

"'Oh, yes?' said her husband, sitting beside her in the car he had just brought to a seat-belt-tightening stop." —*RULES, REGS, AND ROTTEN EGGS* (2007) BY H. R. F. KEATING

COP TALK: MAD AS HELL

Judge Daniel Phelan: *I hold you in contempt, Detective!*
James "Jimmy" McNulty: *Who doesn't?*
—DOMINIC WEST AS DETECTIVE JAMES "JIMMY" MCNULTY AND PETER GERETY AS JUDGE DANIEL PHELAN IN *THE WIRE* (2002–2008)

Career Change or Plot Twist? Same Difference

What's a prosecutor to do after he's spent eleven years prosecuting violent offenders and lecturing nationally on gangs, guns, and crime prevention? He should write about it. This is exactly what Raffi Yessayan, former chief of the Gang Unit in Boston's Suffolk County, has done and with just two legal thrillers released, his name is already being kicked around as the rightful successor to Robert B. Parker. Yessayan's novels are packed with what readers would expect in a good legal thriller/police procedural: great legal twists, bustling courtrooms, top-notch detective work, and murders that the Halls of Justice can't seem to bring before the bar.

∾ *First Lines*

"Richter slipped his arm down the cool shaft of the dryer vent, feeling the dampness of the metal through the latex glove. He slid the bolt lock, gave the door a shove and was inside. Locking the door behind him, he reattached the dryer hose to the vent cover. Let the police work a little to find out how he'd gotten in." —8 IN THE BOX (2008) BY RAFFI YESSAYAN

Wrath in the Bath and Lust at the Prom

Yessayan's first novel, *8 in the Box* (2008), introduces Boston Detective Angel Alves, who's been assigned the task of catching Boston's latest serial killer, known as the Blood Bath Killer. The killer has earned this wrathful moniker because he drains the blood out of his victims in the bathtub.

Yessayan's second book, *2 in the Hat* (2010), finds Angel Alves now looking for the notorious Prom Night Killer, who seems to have returned after a ten-year hiatus, intent on thwarting youthful lust.

In the Tradition of Higgins and Turow

New York Times number-one bestselling author of *The French Connection* (1969), Robin Moore, called Yessayan the best prosecutor-turned-crime-writer since George V. Higgins and Scott Turow. Big shoes to fill, but thus far, Yessayan shows no signs of stumbling.

> *"Anger is a killing thing: it kills the man who angers, for each rage leaves him less than he had been before—it takes something from him."*
> —LOUIS L'AMOUR

Bible Bedtime Stories: Seventy Sons

Jehu was an army captain who led a coup against Jezebel's son, Jehoram, and then dispatched the infamous queen mother. He then commanded that the heads of all seventy of the king's sons be sent to him. Order obeyed.

> *"Anger and intolerance are the enemies of correct understanding."*
> —MOHANDAS GANDHI

The Top Five Odd-Couple Partners

There are the loner cops ("Dirty" Harry Callahan), the ensemble cops (*Barney Miller*), and then there are the buddy cops. The engine that drives the buddy-cop movie is the friction between paired partners who have nothing in common except the badge.

1. *In the Heat of the Night* (1967). Sidney Poitier plays smooth, educated, African American Detective Virgil Tibbs from Philadelphia and Rod Steiger plays good-old Southern boy Police Chief Bill Gillespie of Sparta, Mississippi.
2. *Beverly Hills Cop* (1984). Eddie Murphy plays loose cannon Detroit Detective Axel Foley and John Aston and Judge Reinhold play by-the-book Beverly Hills officers Sergeant John Taggart and Detective Billy Rosewood.

3. *Lethal Weapon* (1987). Mel Gibson plays suicidal widower Sergeant Martin Riggs and Danny Glover plays veteran cop and family man Detective Roger Murtaugh.
4. *Tango & Cash* (1989). Sylvester Stallone plays smooth Lieutenant Ray Tango and Kurt Russell plays shaggy Lieutenant Gabriel Cash.
5. *Bad Boys* (1995). Will Smith plays bachelor Detective Mike Lowery and Martin Lawrence plays family man Detective Marcus Burnett.

COP TALK: MAD AS HELL

Riggs: *We're back, we're bad, you're black, I'm mad.*
—MEL GIBSON AS SERGEANT MARTIN RIGGS IN *LETHAL WEAPON 2* (1989)

"Anybody can become angry—that is easy, but to be angry with the right person and to the right degree and at the right time and for the right purpose, and in the right way—that is not within everybody's power and is not easy." —ARISTOTLE

Anger Management 101

Think cool heads always prevail? Not so fast. Believe it or not, Erle Stanley Gardner, creator of the ever-cool and composed criminal defense attorney Perry Mason, had a wee bit of a temper. In his teens Gardner took up boxing for money and even promoted some unlicensed fights. It seems the young Gentleman Jim upstart took his pugilistic apprenticeship a little too seriously when he left the ring for higher education. By Gardner's own account, he was booted from college for punching out one of his professors. Looks like the experience ultimately convinced him there was a bigger purse in cross-examinations than a quick cross with the right.

COP TALK: MAD AS HELL

Chief Gillespie: *Just once in my life, I'm gonna own my temper. I'm telling you that you're gonna stay here. You're gonna stay here if I have to go inside and call your chief of police and have him remind you of what he told you to do. But I don't think I have to do that, you see?*

—ROD STEIGER AS CHIEF GILLESPIE IN *IN THE HEAT OF THE NIGHT* (1967)

It Takes Two to Murder

Some of history's most notorious killers are tag teams made up of buddies, colleagues, and/or lovers. How many of these deadly duos can you identify? Earn extra points if you know these killing teams by moniker:

1. Hillside Strangler
2. Human Ghoul
3. Lonely Hearts Killers
4. The Moors Murderers
5. Beltway Sniper

a. Martha & Raymond Fernandez
b. Kenneth Bianchi & Angelo Buono
c. Ian Brady & Myra Hindley
d. Sweeney Todd & Margery Lovett
e. John Allen Muhammad & Lee Boyd Malvo

ANSWERS: 1-b; 2-d; 3-a; 4-c; 5-e

❦ *First Lines*

"What Derek Strange was worried about, looking at Jimmy Simmons sitting there, spilling over a chair on the other side of his desk, was that Simmons was going to pick some of Strange's personal shit up off the desktop in front of him and start winging it across the room." —*RIGHT AS RAIN* (2001) BY GEORGE P. PELECANOS

The Quotable P.I. _____

He lied to me. Now I can't think of one reason big enough for him to lie about that's small enough not to matter. —CASEY AFFLECK AS P.I. PATRICK KENZIE IN *GONE BABY GONE* (2007)

Bible Bedtime Stories: Revenge of the She Bears

The Old Testament has many a strange and disconcerting episode. None more so than the following warning to all children not to make fun of the elderly, particularly the follicle challenged elderly:

> *"From there Elisha went up to Bethel. While he was on his way, some small boys came out of the city and jeered at him. "Go up baldhead," they shouted, "go up baldhead!" The prophet turned and saw them, and he cursed them in the name of the Lord. Then two she bears came out of the woods and tore forty-two of the children to pieces."* —2 KINGS 2:23–24 NAB

✺ *First Lines*

"The compiler of this work is of opinion that this book can not have a better introduction to the public than by giving place to the following observations by a highly talented gentleman of this city:

"In hopes that these remarks may meet the attention of many who have hitherto considered it an innocent gratification to witness the death of a fellow being by hanging, they are respectfuly offered to the public." —*THE RECORD OF CRIMES IN THE UNITED STATES; CONTAINING A BRIEF SKETCH OF THE PROMINENT TRAITS IN THE CHARACTER AND CONDUCT OF MANY OF THE MOST NOTORIOUS MALEFACTORS, WHO HAVE BEEN GUILTY OF CAPITAL OFFENSES; AND WHO HAVE BEEN DETECTED AND CONVICTED* (1834) "COMPILED FROM THE BEST AUTHORITIES," EDITED BY JAMES FAXON

> *"Other sins only speak; murder shrieks out*
> *The element of water moistens the earth,*
> *But blood flies upwards, and bedews the heavens."*
> —JOHN WEBSTER, *THE DUCHESS OF MALFI*

The Quotable P.I.

Lew Harper: *The bottom is loaded with nice people, Albert. Only cream and bastards rise.* —PAUL NEWMAN AS P.I. LEW HARPER IN *HARPER* (1966)

Destination: Murder

Adelaide, Australia, has gotten a bad rap as "The City of Corpses." Known first as "The City of Churches," a wave of grisly murders in and around Adelaide stretching back through the 1950s has left some less focused on the city's architecture. Notorious crimes on Adelaide's rap sheet include:

- The rape and murder of nine-year-old Mary Hattam in 1958
- The unsolved 1966 disappearances of Jane, Arnna, and Grant Beaumont, ages nine, seven, and four
- The 1971 execution of ten members of the Bartholomew family
- Dr. George Duncan's murder by drowning in 1972
- The unsolved disappearances of Joanne Ratcliffe, seventeen, and Kristy Gordon, four, in 1973
- The Truro murders (1978–1979), which left seven women dead
- The murder of lawyer Derrance Stevenson in 1979
- The 1979–1983 deaths and mutilations of five young men, ages fifteen to twenty-five

- The letter-bombing of Adelaide's offices of National Crime Authority in 1994
- The eight Snowtown Murder victims discovered in barrels, plus four others found buried, in 1999

> "A tourist booklet for Adelaide, if one wished to capture all of the finer points of the city might read: 'Adelaide, come for the wine, visit the churches, but stay for the murder.'" —WES LAURIE, "ADELAIDE, AUSTRALIA: THE CITY OF CORPSES" (2007)

BLOOD & BONES

"An operation during life is attended by pain and is for the benefit of the individuals. An operation after death is free from pain and is for the benefit of humanity." —BRAOUARDEL & JASOLIN

ᕲ *First Lines*

"By now it's no secret." —*THE BADGE: TRUE AND TERRIFYING CRIME STORIES THAT COULD NOT BE PRESENTED ON TV, FROM THE CREATOR AND STAR OF DRAGNET* (1958) BY JACK WEBB

DEADLY DIALOGUE

"*One day I'll get over that wall of anger, and it will be glorious.*"
—WILL FERRELL AS NYPD DETECTIVE ALLEN GAMBLE IN *THE OTHER GUYS* (2010)

Stranger Than Fiction

Q: What real-life multiple murderer is believed to have been a model for these three fictional killers: Norman Bates (*Psycho*), Buffalo Bill (*Silence of the Lambs*), and Leatherface (*Texas Chainsaw Massacre*)?

A: Edward Gein (1906–1984) of Wisconsin started robbing graves and later killed at least two women for body parts, which he used to make grisly artifacts, including a "woman suit." Found among his collection were face masks, leggings, and a vest made of human skin. Gein also sealed off part of his house as a shrine to his overly protective and possessive mother. He was deemed legally insane, but later was tried and convicted on one count of murder. He spent the rest of his life in mental institutions.

> *"To his friends and neighbors, he was only a handyman and a most dependable and trustworthy babysitter."* —ROBERT BLOCH, "THE SHAMBLES OF ED GEIN" (1962)

The Butcher's Cut

London's Whitechapel murders of 1888–1891 may be the best known unsolved cases in history—if only because Jack the Ripper stands accused of committing them. Eleven murders in two years have been connected to Jack's infamous name, but after more than a century, the suspect list is still more than a hundred names long. Some experts believe that Jack the Ripper's *modus operandi*—prostitutes found with their throats cut before being mutilated and disemboweled—points to a doctor or butcher. But with a case this cold, it's possible that we may never know for sure.

Copycat Murders: Jack the Stripper

While Jack the Ripper is one of the most famous unknown killers, there have been other unsolved crimes that seem to mirror the Ripper's. For instance, London had a series of eerily similar murders between 1964–1965. Jack the Stripper was the nickname given to an unknown serial killer responsible for what came to be known as the London "nude murders."

Ripper: Stripper

- Similarity #1: His victims, like Jack the Ripper's, were prostitutes. He murdered six, and possibly eight prostitutes, whose nude bodies were discovered around London or dumped in the River Thames. The victim count is ambiguous because two of the murders attributed to him did not fit his *modus operandi*.

- Similarity #2: Like the Jack the Ripper killings, the Stripper's reign of terror seemed to cease on its own, and there were few solid clues for police to investigate.

Who Was Jack the Stripper?

The main suspect, who was also a favorite suspect of Chief Superintendent Du Rose, was a security guard on the Heron Trading Estate in Acton, whose rounds included a paint shop where one of the bodies was thought to have been hidden after the crime. Though there was never any hard evidence to link him to the crimes, his family found his suicide inexplicable, and his suicide note cryptically said only that he was "unable to take the strain any longer."

"Anger is like a full-hot horse, who being allow'd his way, self-mettle tires him." —SHAKESPEARE

The Axeman Appears

On May 23, 1918, an Italian grocer named Joseph Maggio and his wife were butchered while sleeping in their apartment above their grocery store. Upon investigation, the police discovered a panel in the rear door had been chiseled out, providing a way in for the killer. The murder weapon, an axe, was found in the apartment, still coated with the Maggios' blood. Nothing in the house had been stolen, though jewelry and money were nearly in plain sight. The only clue was a message written in chalk near the victims' home: "Mrs. Joseph Maggio will sit up tonight. Just write Mrs. Toney."

Copycat Murders: The Axeman of New Orleans

The Axeman murdered a total of eight people, the murders both brutal and apparently random. His victims included a pregnant woman and even a baby killed in the arms of its mother.

To Rip or to Axe . . .

- Similarity #1: In imitation of Jack the Ripper, the Axeman (or someone claiming to be the Axeman) wrote taunting letters to city newspapers hinting at his future crimes and claiming to be a demon from hell.

  Not everyone was intimidated by the Axeman. Some well-armed citizens sent the newspaper invitations for the Axeman to visit their houses that night and see who got killed first. One invitation promised to leave a window open for the Axeman, politely asking that he not damage the front door.

- Similarity #2: Though there were three more attacks after his first appearance, the last on October 27, 1919, the murders stopped suddenly and the crimes remain unsolved.

Jazz Rx for the Serial Killer's Soul

On March 13, 1919, a letter from the Axeman was published in the newspapers saying that he would kill again at fifteen minutes past midnight on March 19, but would spare the occupants of any place where a jazz band was playing. That night all of the New Orleans dance halls were filled to capacity, and professional and amateur bands played jazz at parties at hundreds of houses around town. There were no murders that night.

COP TALK: MAD AS HELL

Harry Callahan: *Go ahead, make my day.*
—CLINT EASTWOOD AS INSPECTOR "DIRTY" HARRY CALLAHAN IN *SUDDEN IMPACT* (1983)

KILLER WIT

"The best way to do it is with scissors."
—ALFRED HITCHCOCK

ENVY

n., via Old French from the Latin *invidere*, meaning to look at with envy

1. Covetousness; jealousy
2. Begrudging of another's qualities or possessions
3. The object of such a begrudging

"Envy, like the worm, never runs but to the fairest fruit; like a cunning bloodhound, it singles out the fattest deer in the flock." **—FRANCIS BEAUMONT**

The emphasis placed on envy in the Ten Commandments—*You shall not covet your neighbor's house. You shall not covet your neighbor's wife, or his male or female servant, his ox or donkey, or anything that belongs to your neighbor*—speaks to the perils of this pernicious emotion. (Not to mention that as this list concludes the commandments, God apparently saved the best—or should we say worst—for last.) Beware the envier—and to the envied, be scared!

> *"Of the seven deadly sins, only envy is no fun at all."* —JOSEPH EPSTEIN

The Hierarchy of Cop Envy

- Patrol officers want to be sergeants.
- Sergeants want to be lieutenants.
- Lieutenants want to be captains.
- Captains want to be chief.
- The chief wants to be a simple patrol officer.

COP TALK: AT THE PRECINCT

Detective James "Jimmy" McNulty: *I wonder what it feels like to work in a real police department!*

—DOMINIC WEST AS DETECTIVE JAMES "JIMMY" MCNULTY IN *THE WIRE* (2002–2008)

Name That Theme Song

Cop show theme songs are the envy of every other form of television entertainment. Match the popular theme song to the composer:

1. *Miami Vice*	**a.** Earle H. Hagen
2. *Swat*	**b.** Morton Stevens
3. *The Andy Griffith Show*	**c.** Walter Schumann
4. *Dragnet*	**d.** Jan Hammer
5. *Hill Street Blues*	**e.** Mike Post
6. *Hawaii Five-O*	**f.** Barry DeVorzon with Rhythm Heritage

ANSWERS: 1-d; 2-f; 3-a; 4-c; 5-e; 6-b

KILLER WIT
"Television has brought murder back into the home—where it belongs."
—ALFRED HITCHCOCK

COP TALK: AT THE PRECINCT
Vincent Hanna: *So you never wanted a regular type life?*
—AL PACINO AS LIEUTENANT VINCENT HANNA IN *HEAT* (1995)

Private Dick Envy: Winners
The magic number is, apparently, eight.

- Mike Conners played Joe Mannix (*Mannix*, 1967–1975) for eight years.
- Tom Selleck played Thomas Magnum (*Magnum, P.I.*, 1980–1988) for eight years.
- Gerald McRaney played Richard "Rick" Simon and Jameson Parker played Andrew Jackson "A. J." Simon (*Simon & Simon*, 1981–1989) for eight years.

Ratings to Die For
Just a little envious are these runners-up.

- Buddy Ebsen played Barnaby Jones (*Barnaby Jones*, 1973–1980) for seven years.
- Efrem Zimbalist Jr. played Stuart "Stu" Bailey and Roger Smith played Jeff Spencer (*77 Sunset Strip*, 1958–1964) for six years.
- William Conrad played Frank Cannon (*Cannon*, 1971–1976), which ran for five years and spun off *Barnaby Jones*.

That Hail Mary Pass Isn't All We Envy

Match the law enforcement professionals that quarterback-turned-actor Mark Harmon has played with uncommon success in TV shows over the past thirty years:

1. Los Angeles police officer Mike Breen

2. Deputy Dwayne "Thib" Thibideaux

3. Chicago police detective Dicky Cobb

4. Supervisory Special Agent Leroy Jethro Gibbs

a. *Reasonable Doubts 3* (1991–1993)

b. *Sam* (1978)

c. *NCIS* (2003–)

d. *240-Robert* (1979–1980)

ANSWERS: 1-b; 2-d; 3-a; 4-c

ℜ *First Lines*

"*It's when you're going good that they throw at your head.*" —*STRIKE THREE, YOU'RE DEAD* (1984) BY R. D. ROSEN

Private Dick Envy: Losers

Who can blame the following for feeling envious? They didn't last more than a year.

- Edmond O'Brien played Johnny Midnight (*Johnny Midnight*, 1960).
- Ben Vereen played E. L. (Early Leroy) "Tenspeed" Turner and Jeff Goldblum played Lionel "Brown Shoe" Whitney (*Tenspeed and Brown Shoe*, 1980).
- Dennis Dugan played Richie Brockelman (*Richie Brockelman, Private Eye*, 1978).
- Tim Daly played Harlan Judd (*Eyes*, 2005).

The mean streets have nothing on the ratings.

KILLER WIT

"Disney has the best casting. If he doesn't like an actor he just tears him up."
—ALFRED HITCHCOCK

The Quotable P.I.

"Try this for a deep, dark secret: the great detective, Remington Steele? He doesn't exist. I invented him. Follow. I always loved excitement, so I studied, and apprenticed, and put my name on an office. But absolutely nobody knocked down my door. A female private investigator seemed so . . . feminine. So I invented a superior. A decidedly masculine superior. Suddenly there were cases around the block. It was working like a charm . . . until the day HE walked in, with his blue eyes and mysterious past. And before I knew it, he assumed Remington Steele's identity. Now I do the work, and he takes the bows. It's a dangerous way to live, but as long as people buy it, I can get the job done. We never mix business with pleasure. Well, almost never. I don't even know his real name!" —STEPHANIE ZIMBALIST AS LAURA HOLT IN *REMINGTON STEELE* (1982–1987)

A Wolf Takes on the Seven Deadly Sins

God may have created the world in seven days, but artistic creator Dick Wolf created perhaps the most successful marketing strategy of the seven deadly sins since the serpent in the Garden: the mega-successful *Law & Order* franchise.

The inaugural *Law & Order* series first aired in September 1990. Plots are ripped from the current most shocking headlines, many horrific and bizarre murder motives: lust, greed, envy, and more. Whatever headlines had to offer on human frailty became fair game for Wolf.

Cops & Lawyers, The One-Two Punch

Q: From which early 1960s show does *Law & Order* borrow its unique structure?

A: Ben Gazzara and Chuck Connors starred in *Arrest & Trial*, which aired only one season, 1963–1964. As with its successor, the first half of the show dealt with the police investigation and the second half with the prosecution. It's a formula for success.

Law & Order . . . Again

Law & Order birthed at least three spinoffs:

1. *Law & Order: Criminal Intent*
2. *Law & Order: Special Victims Unit* (dealing with victims of sex crimes)
3. *Law & Order: Trial by Jury*

The original *Law & Order* was cancelled after some twenty seasons, becoming one of the longest-running prime-time shows in history. The original show set in New York was swiftly replaced by *Law & Order: Los Angeles*—now that's sinful.

> *"It's show business. No show, no business."* —DICK WOLF, CREATOR OF *LAW & ORDER*

There's Only One Top Cop

Q: What's the top-grossing cop film of all time?

A: According to the *Wall Street Journal* ("Reel Dollars," January 30, 2010), *Beverly Hills Cop* (1984) is the highest-grossing cop film, with a domestic gross of $234,760,478 (or $521,224,157, adjusted for inflation at the time of the article). Eddie Murphy went on to play Detective Axel Foley two more times, in *Beverly Hills Cop 2* (1987) and *Beverly Hills Cop 3* (1994).

Because Life Imitates Art (and Bad Movies)

The Motion Picture Production Code (AKA the Hays Code) was an attempt by the Motion Pictures Producers and Distributors Association (MPPDA) to keep audiences from being seduced by an easy life of crime.

According to the code, movies were not allowed to:

1. Teach methods of crime.
2. Inspire potential criminals with a desire for imitation.
3. Make criminals seem heroic and justified.

ℜ *First Lines*

"Sheriff Dan Rhodes wasn't sure why the Blacklin County Sheriff's Department needed an M-16.

"Commissioner Mickey Burns was happy to explain. 'Firepower,' he said. His eyes gleamed. 'Nine hundred and fifty rounds a minute. The bullets travel at twenty-nine hundred feet per second. Can you believe that? Punch a hole in a tank with something like that.'" —*MURDER IN THE AIR* (2010) BY BILL CRIDER

Do You Wish You Could Get Away?

Let these authors be your travel agents.

- Martin Cruz Smith uses detective Arkady Renko to take you on a tour of Russia, the Arctic Circle, and Cuba, starting with *Gorky Park* (1981).
- Donna Leon uses Commissario Guido Brunetti to take you on a tour of Venice, starting with *Death at La Fenice* (1992).
- Qiu Xiaolong uses Chief Inspector Chen Cao to take you on a tour of China, starting with *Death of a Red Heroine* (2000).

- Luiz Alfredo Garcia-Roza uses Inspector Espinosa to take you on a tour of Rio de Janeiro, starting with *The Silence of the Rain* (2002).
- Michael Chabon uses Detective Meyer Landsman to take you on a tour of an alternative reality where Alaska is a Jewish settlement in *The Yiddish Policemen's Union* (2007).

"I Think We're Gonna Need a Bigger Boat"

In 1974, ex-con Buck Walker and his girlfriend Stephanie Stearns were stuck on Palmyra Atoll, 1,200 miles from Hawaii, with dwindling supplies and just a rickety wooden sloop to get them to the next supply port. What should sail into the harbor, but a beautiful, fully supplied ketch, *Sea Wind*, manned only by yacht enthusiasts Mac and Muff Graham.

When Walker and Stearns were caught with the repainted and renamed ketch, they claimed they found the Grahams' dinghy overturned in the surf and searched for the missing couple for more than a week. Then, well, they just took the boat. Both were convicted of theft.

In 1981, the burnt and dismembered remains of Muff Graham were found next to a large chest in the surf off Palmyra Atoll. Walker and Stearns were tried separately for murder; he was convicted and she was acquitted. Mac's body was never found.

◎ *First Lines*

"Maui, Hawaii

"April 1, 1974

"It had rained during the night, one of those warm tropical showers that leaves the air heavy and sweet."

—*AND THE SEA WILL TELL* (1991) BY VINCENT BUGLIOSI AND BRUCE B. HENDERSON

Why Every Police Officer Really Wants to Be a Private Investigator

Cops envy private investigators their not having to deal with bureaucracy, their ability to choose what jobs they're going to accept, and their high hourly rate.

Live the Life of a P.I.—The Envy of Every Mild-Mannered Accountant

Do you dream about being a private investigator? It doesn't have to be a pipe dream—depending on where you live.

Most states require licensing, and some go so far as to administer tests. But not all.

If you don't live in Colorado, Idaho, Mississippi, South Dakota, or Wyoming, don't you wish you did? People living in these five states can simply call themselves private investigators to make it true.

> *"Why all this devotion to a man who was intensely prejudiced, imperious, often bad-tempered, thoughtless with people who might look to him for a little kindness, capable of an unmerited snub, grossly self-indulgent, arrogant, opinionated—and decidedly touchy about trivialities? Well, just because he is Sherlock Holmes. (And in our imaginations we are Sherlock Holmes!)"* —VINCENT PRICE

Read 'Em and Weep

If you've always wanted to live the life of a gumshoe, check out the following:

- *All Grass Isn't Green* (1970) by A. A. Fair
- "All I Want for Christmas Is My Two Front Teeth" (2006) by Lori Avocato

- *Blue Shoes and Happiness* (2006) by Alexander McCall Smith
- *Dreaming of Babylon* (1977) by Richard G. Brautigan
- *Easy As One, Two, Three* (1999) by Phillip DePoy
- *Every Bet's a Sure Thing* (1953) by Thomas B. Dewey
- *It Isn't Easy Being Johnny Style* (2003) by Patrick K. Jassoy
- *The Kubla Khan Caper* (1966) by Richard S. Prather
- *The Small Boat of Great Sorrows* (2003) by Dan Fesperma
- *The Sure Thing* (1975) by Richard S. Prather

We Don't Need No Stinking Badges!

Believing that the private eye novel was being given short shrift by the other mystery organizations, Robert J. Randisi founded the Private Eye Writers of America in 1981. PWA awards the Shamus Awards for the best works of P.I. fiction.

Why Every Private Investigator Really Wants to Be a Police Officer

Private investigators envy cops their guaranteed salary, their benefits, and their ability to tap into official databases.

The Other Woman

The biggest mystery in master storyteller Agatha Christie's real life took place in 1926, when she disappeared for eleven days. When her car was found abandoned in Surrey with her fur coat and suitcase still inside, it caused an international sensation. A high-profile search ensued, while Christie hid out in an out-of-the-way hotel under her cheating husband Archie's lover's name, apparently suffering an envy-induced nervous breakdown. She and Archie were divorced two years later, and Archie married his mistress, Nancy Neele.

Christie later married the noted archaeologist Max Mallowan, a union that proved far happier than her first.

Dirty Laundry, Silver Screen

In the 1979 movie *Agatha*, inspired by the incident, Vanessa Redgrave played Christie and Dustin Hoffman played Wally Stanton, the fictional American journalist who realizes who she is and sets out to help her.

"I Don't Brake for Cheats"

Running over a cheating husband once might be an accident and some might even say understandable. But Clara Harris was charged with murder in 2002 for repeatedly driving her Mercedes-Benz over her husband, David, in the parking lot of the Houston hotel where she'd confronted him about his infidelity. Clara got twenty years. Save your sympathy for David Harris's sixteen-year-old daughter, who was in the car when her stepmother ran down her dad.

> *"A man who has never made a woman angry is a failure in life."*
> —CHRISTOPHER MORLEY

What the King Covets

You'd think a humble shepherd boy would be content to become first the hero of his people and then king of Israel with a harem full of wives and concubines. But David, who slew the mighty Goliath, fell for another man's wife just like he'd been socked between the eyes with a rock from his own slingshot.

David was wandering about the roof of his palace in Jerusalem while his troops were off ravaging and besieging the usual enemies. He spied a lovely young woman bathing on a rooftop below, who turned out to be married to one of his top soldiers. David sent for Bathsheba (apparently forgetting that commandment about not coveting his neighbor's wife) and got her pregnant. Hoping to avert a scandal, David recalled Uriah, the husband, from the battlefield and tried to get him to go home and sleep with his wife. Uriah, however, insisted on saving his strength for battle. David opted for Plan B: murder.

> *"In the morning David wrote a letter to Joab, [his commander], and sent it with Uriah. In it he wrote, 'Put Uriah out in front where the fighting is fiercest. Then withdraw from him so he will be struck down and die.'"*
> —2 SAMUEL 11:14–15 NIV

The Sins of the Fathers

Soon after Uriah's death, David married Bathsheba. He got called on his perfidy by the prophet Nathan, who told him "the sword shall never depart from your house." David repented, but at least four of his sons met bad ends, two at the hands of their brothers.

In David's old age, Bathsheba maneuvered him into declaring her son, Solomon, as the next king and she was honored as a sort of "Queen Mum" of the Israelites.

BLOOD & BONES

"You will acquire a deep understanding of that ancient Christian moral principle, as applied to aimed fire, 'It is better to give than to receive.'"
—GEORGE PROSSER

The Mother-in-Law from Hell

Frank Duncan had a burden to bear in his mother's domineering, manipulative, possessive ways. What other lawyer, in California, no less, had to contend with a mother who attended all his court appearances and applauded when he won? A serial bigamist who passed bad checks and lied, all the time and about everything?

She wasn't above faking a suicide attempt to get her way either. And that's when the real trouble started. Elizabeth Duncan was determined not to share her only son with anyone, especially not Olga Kupczyk, the attractive nurse Frank met at her hospital bedside. She opposed their marriage, even though Olga was pregnant, so the couple wed in secret. Mother Duncan then hired two young men to kill her daughter-in-law.

When the deed was done and the body buried in a makeshift grave, Elizabeth not only refused to pay most of what she had promised: She complained to the police that the two men were blackmailing her! All three were sent to the gas chamber in 1962.

"Adam was the luckiest man; he had no mother-in-law." —MARK TWAIN

How to Kill Your Mother-in-Law (Proven Weapons from Real Crimes)

- Rocket launcher
- Machine gun
- Ice pick
- Rope
- Fire
- Handgun
- Golf ball

> "O! beware, my lord, of jealousy;
> It is the green-eyed monster which doth mock
> The meat it feeds on."
>
> —*OTHELLO* BY WILLIAM SHAKESPEARE

That Magnifying Glass Brings Out the Color of Your Eyes

Q: Which Nancy Drew novel is all about the green-eyed monster?

A: Well, there is *Green-Eyed Monster*, billed as Book One of the Eco Mystery Trilogy. But there's also *Green with Envy*, billed as Book Two of the Eco Mystery Trilogy. And the monster is still peeking around corners in Book Three of the Eco Mystery Trilogy, *Seeing Green*. Things have changed since *The Secret of the Old Clock*—there's all kinds of green now!

The Color of Murder

Jealousy is a motive much preferred by many mystery writers including:

- *The Case of the Green-Eyed Sister* (1953) by Erle Stanley Gardner
- *The Green-Eyed Monster* (1960) by Patrick Quentin
- *Modesty Blaise: The Green-Eyed Monster* (graphic novel) (2005) by Peter O'Donnell and Enric Badia Romero
- *Green-Eyed Demon* (2011) by Jaye Wells
- *Demons of the Green Eyed Monster* (2008) by Edward Donohue

Fickle Finger-Pointing of Fate

In 1994, Susan Smith of South Carolina claimed a black man carjacked her and drove off with her two sons, Michael and Alexander. Nine days later she confessed to sending the car, with her two little boys strapped in their seats, down a ramp and into a lake. Smith and her husband were getting a divorce, and she hoped to "trade up" and marry a wealthy lover who had dumped her, saying among other things that he didn't want to raise her children.

> *"Jealousy, as it so often does, throws open the door to murder."* —HERCULE POIROT IN *THE MYSTERY OF THE BLUE TRAIN* (2005) BY AGATHA CHRISTIE

Bigger, Better, Classier?

Q: The investment and social club, BBC Consolidated, Inc., was better-known by what nickname?

A: The Billionaire Boys Club. Members of the club founded by Joseph Gamsky, AKA Joe Hunt, were implicated in the murder of shady businessman Ron Levin and the kidnapping and death of Hedayat Eslaminia, the father of one of the club members. Hunt spent the money he charmed out of investors on a lavish lifestyle for the young men in the BBC, including ten matching motorcycles. He and the club's "head of security" were convicted of trying to force money out of Levin at gunpoint (the check was no good), then killing him.

> *"Joe's method was to instill in them an all-encompassing desire for flashy cars, beautiful girls, and classy living so that they'd go along with anything he did, including murder."* —KATHERINE RAMSLAND, "JOE HUNT: WHITE COLLAR PSYCHOPATH"

Step One: Tape Mouth

Levin's body was never found, but Hunt's seven-page list of steps for carrying out the murder was left at the scene. (He did remember to "take the holes"—the paper circles left when he hole-punched falsified papers to add to Levin's files.) In 1992, Hunt was sentenced to life without chance of parole. Two other club members were convicted in the Eslaminia case (one was later overturned). Hunt represented himself, got a hung jury, and the case was dismissed.

> "(1) Tape mouth
> (2) Close blinds
> (3) Handcuff—put gloves on
> (10) Kill dog"
> —FROM JOE HUNT'S LIST FOUND AT RON LEVIN'S HOME

BBC Membership Test

Q: Would you murder someone, if you knew you could get away with it, for a million dollars?

Q: Would you do it if it were a matter of saving your life?

Q: Would you murder someone if you had to do it to save your mother?

If you answered "yes" to any of the above, Hunt would say (as was testified at Hunt's murder trial), "Then you can't claim that you have a line you won't cross."

The Bible's First Murder

While wrath and avarice seem to be the major murder motives, the very first murder was apparently motivated by none other than envy. According to the Bible:

"And Adam knew Eve his wife; and she conceived, and bare Cain, and said, I have gotten a man from the Lord. And she again bare his brother Abel. And Abel was a keeper of sheep, but Cain was a tiller of the ground. And in process of time it came to pass, that Cain brought of the fruit of the ground an offering unto the Lord. And Abel, he also brought of the firstlings of his flock and of the fat thereof. And the Lord had respect unto Abel and to his offering: But unto Cain and to his offering he had not respect. And Cain was very wroth, and his countenance fell. And the Lord said unto Cain, Why art thou wroth? and why is thy countenance fallen? If thou doest well, shalt thou not be accepted? and if thou doest not well, sin lieth at the door. And unto thee shall be his desire, and thou shalt rule over him. And Cain talked with Abel his brother: and it came to pass, when they were in the field, that Cain rose up against Abel his brother, and slew him. And the Lord said unto Cain, Where is Abel thy brother? And he said, I know not: Am I my brother's keeper? And he said, What hast thou done? the voice of thy brother's blood crieth unto me from the ground. And now art thou cursed from the earth, which hath opened her mouth to receive thy brother's blood from thy hand; when thou tillest the ground, it shall not henceforth yield unto thee her strength; a fugitive and a vagabond shalt thou be in the earth. And Cain said unto the Lord, My punishment is greater than I can bear. Behold, thou hast driven me out this day from the face of the earth; and from thy face shall I be hid; and I shall be a fugitive and a vagabond in the earth; and it shall come to pass, that every one that findeth me shall slay me. And the Lord said unto him, Therefore whosoever slayeth Cain, vengeance shall be taken on him sevenfold. And the Lord set a mark upon Cain, lest any finding him should kill him. And Cain went out from the presence of the Lord, and dwelt in the land of Nod, on the east of Eden."

This is the King James Version. There are other variations on the theme, but envy seems the prime motivator.

> *"The jealous are troublesome to others, but a torment to themselves."*
> —WILLIAM PENN

ଡ଼ *First Lines*

"Saturday night. It was not a night to be spending alone, riding a bus. When he was a teenager at the comprehensive, Saturday night without a girl, without a date, without at least your mates to raise hell with, Saturday night alone would have been shameful." —THE STARGAZEY (1999)
BY MARTHA GRIMES

Prosecuting the Prosecutor

Q: Which 1987 novel about a Chicago prosecutor is often called the first real legal thriller?
A: *Presumed Innocent,* by Scott Turow. Eight-time bestselling novelist Scott Turow will tell audiences that he did not create the legal thriller, but he certainly ignited a *tour de force* genre with the 1987 release of the suspenseful, plot-driven, character-driven courtroom drama novel that became a runaway bestseller, selling millions of copies.

Going Hollywood

In the 1990 movie version of *Presumed Innocent,* Harrison Ford stars as Turow's protagonist, Rusty Sabich. Sabich is a married, middle-aged chief deputy prosecutor in a midwestern county. His former paramour, the beautiful, intelligent, and seductive colleague Carolyn Polehemus, ends up murdered and the DA hands Sabich the assignment of bringing her killer before the bar. Sabich is tormented by her murder, their past, and his ethical dilemma as chief prosecutor and former lover. Ultimately, he is fingered as her killer. His friend the DA has abandoned him. His colleagues and society shun him. He is in the legal battle of his life to save his marriage, family, freedom, and reputation. Envy, greed, and lust are just a few of the seven deadly sins lying in wait to bring Sabich to his knees.

> *"On the streets, unrequited love and death go together almost as often as in Shakespeare."* —SCOTT TUROW

It's All about the Innocent

Name Scott Turow's long-awaited sequel to *Presumed Innocent*.

ANSWER: *Innocent* was released in 2010 to excellent reviews.

When Power and Envy Corrupt

Q: What series written by former prosecutor George V. Higgins features a Boston criminal defense attorney who doesn't always hold prosecutors in high regard?

A: Jerry Kennedy, like Higgins, is a Boston Irish Catholic who represents the type of lower-echelon hoods featured so often in Higgins's street-wise, gritty novels. The Kennedy novels see things from the defense attorney's perspective, which is surprising since Higgins was a top-notch U.S. Attorney who was very proud of his record prosecuting the anti-hero types featured in his works. In contrast to Higgins, Kennedy sometimes views prosecutors as overzealous and drunk on power, and willing to let pride and envy overshadow procedural due process. Higgins made it very clear, however, that this is Kennedy's take on prosecutors and not his.

Kennedy Canon

- *Kennedy for the Defense* (1980)
- *Penance for Jerry Kennedy* (1985)
- *Defending Billy Ryan* (1992)
- *Sandra Nichols Found Dead* (1996)

> *"There are many things that we would throw away if we were not afraid that others might pick them up."* —OSCAR WILDE

Character Envy

Can a man be envious of himself? Arthur Train, creator of Yankee lawyer Ephraim Tutt—the onetime "best known lawyer in America"—had a bit of an identity crisis. Train would lament that his author friends thought of him as a lawyer who wrote, and his lawyer friends thought of him as a writer who practiced law. The truth is, Train mastered both vocations. A Harvard undergrad and Harvard Law grad, Train worked for many years as an assistant district attorney in New York City and was a superb trial attorney.

> *"A person is born with feelings of envy and hate. If he gives way to them, they will lead him to violence and crime, and any sense of loyalty and good faith will be abandoned."* —XUNZI

King Tutt

In 1919 Arthur Train created the lovable, old fox of a lawyer, Mr. Tutt, a forerunner to Perry Mason. Like Mason, Tutt never fails to have a legal trick up his sleeve, yet always uses his adroit skills on the side of the angels. He is always there—usually without charging a fee—to help the widow slated to be foreclosed on by a greedy banker. Or to save innocent maidens from lust-minded men. And to free the young man dragged into the vengeful clutches of a jealous reprobate.

The Tutt stories appear in short story form and are supported by actual case law. The Tutt stories are so sound in law, and how the human element often dictates the application of law, that for many years they became assigned reading in law schools throughout the country—including Harvard! Now that ought to make any lawyer or writer jealous.

> *"Man will do many things to get himself loved, he will do all things to get himself envied."* —MARK TWAIN

BLOOD & BONES

"Many people ask me why I chose Forensic Medicine as a career, and I tell them that it is because a forensic man gets the honor of being called when the top doctors have failed!" —ANIL AGGRAWAL

> *"Love that is fed by jealousy dies hard."* —OVID

PRIDE

n., from the Old English *prud*, meaning proud

- A feeling of self-respect and/or self-worth
- A feeling of gratification stemming from a given achievement, possession, or association
- Arrogant behavior or disdainful conduct
- A source of gratification and/or satisfaction
- A peak or prime condition
- Excessive self-importance
- High-spiritedness in horses
- A group of lions; also a group of peacocks
- An ostentatious or striking group

"Pride goeth before destruction, and an haughty spirit before a fall."
—PROVERBS 16:18 KJV

What the Bible fails to mention is that the first fall that comes as a result of pride is often the victim—or victims—of the proud. Wounded vanity—actual or perceived—is the motive for many a murderer. Only in the most just of outcomes does the proud perpetrator fall as well—and as hard—as the victim.

> *"'Elementary,' said he. 'It is one of those instances where the reasoner can produce an effect which seems remarkable to his neighbour, because the latter has missed the one little point which is the basis of the deduction. The same may be said, my dear fellow, for the effect of some of these little sketches of yours, which is entirely meretricious, depending as it does upon your retaining in your own hands some factors in the problem which are never imparted to the reader.'"* —
> SHERLOCK HOLMES IN "THE CROOKED MAN" (1893) BY SIR ARTHUR
> CONAN DOYLE

COP TALK: MACHISMO SPEAKS!

Thomas Gabriel: *You're very impressed with yourself, aren't you?*

John McClane: *I have my moments.*

—BRUCE WILLIS AS DETECTIVE JOHN MCCLANE AND TIMOTHY OLYPHANT AS THOMAS GABRIEL IN *LIVE FREE OR DIE HARD* (2007)

Sherlock's Mistake

Q: What case proves Conan Doyle's ignorance of herpetology?

A: In "The Speckled Band," Sherlock Holmes solves a locked room mystery—or does he? Helen Stoner tells Sherlock that her sister, Julia, had been sleeping in a locked room when she screamed, ran out into the hall, and yelled, "It was the band! The speckled band!" Then she promptly fell over dead. The sisters lived with their nasty stepfather, Doctor Roylott, in his crumbling ancestral home. He had previously lived in India and he allowed a baboon and a cheetah to wander freely over his estate. (It's never stated what the cheetah ate, but the baboon must have been nervous.) Helen tells Holmes that Julia had earlier mentioned hearing a strange whistle in the night. When Helen died, Julia heard the whistle also.

It turns out that if Julia had just screamed, "It was a snake! It was a goddamn snake that bit me!" Holmes might not have been needed at all. But he figured it out anyway. Roylott had a deadly "Indian swamp adder." He had trained it to go through a small ventilation hole and down a bell-pull rope hanging over Julia's bed. Julia had to die because she was engaged and, when she married, much of her late mother's money would go to her, rather than Roylott. The whistle both girls had heard was Roylott's signal for the snake to slither back up the bell-rope through the ventilation hole, and back to Roylott's room.

The Quotable P.I. ───────────────────────

Daryl Zero: *I can't possibly overstate the importance of good research.*
—BILL PULLMAN AS P.I. DARYL ZERO IN *ZERO EFFECT* (1998)

Snakes on a Rope, circa 2012

A modern detective would have ruined Sherlock's reputation in "The Speckled Band," leaving the crime unsolved. She would have said, "Hell, it can't be an Indian swamp adder. They don't exist. Even if they did, no snake can crawl up or down a bell-rope. I guess the evil doctor could've rubbed some glue on his belly, but then he'd still be hanging from the top of the rope. And whistle? Excuse me? Snakes don't have outer ears. They can only sense vibrations. And from another room? No way. Sorry, Sherlock, but this one ain't as elementary as you think."

COP TALK: MACHISMO SPEAKS!

Harry Callahan: *Well, I just work for the city, Briggs!*

Lieutenant Briggs: *So do I, longer than you, and I never had to take my gun out of its holster once. I'm proud of that.*

Harry Callahan: *Well, you're a good man, lieutenant. A good man always knows his limitations. . .*

—CLINT EASTWOOD AS INSPECTOR "DIRTY" HARRY CALLAHAN AND HAL HOLBROOK AS LIEUTENANT NEIL BRIGGS IN *MAGNUM FORCE* (1973)

A Detective by Any Other Name

Q: Who was the real Sherlock Holmes?

A: Sir Bernard Henry Spilsbury: England's Real Sherlock Holmes

---

"I have never claimed to be God—but merely his locum on his weekends off." —BERNARD SPILSBURY (1877–1947)

The Crippen Case

Considered to be Britain's most famous forensic pathologist, Bernard Spilsbury was brilliant, arrogant, and eccentric. The case that brought him to public attention was the Dr. Crippen case in 1910. Spilsbury concluded that a scar on a small piece of skin from the remains found in Crippen's cellar belonged to his wife, who was planning to leave Crippen and take half of their savings with her.

Dead Brides in the Bath

The case that put Spilsbury on the road to becoming Britain's most famous forensic pathologist was the "Brides in the Bath" murder trial of 1915. Three women had died mysteriously in their baths, in each case the death seeming to be an accident. George Smith was tried for the murder of one of these women—Bessie Mundy. Spilsbury testified that since Bessie's thigh showed evidence of "goose skin," and since she was, in death, clutching a bar of soap, it was certain that she had died a violent death, and in fact had been murdered. The evidence doesn't stand up to scrutiny by modern science, but seemed convincing enough at the time to make Spilsbury seem like a "medical detective," and he became known as a real-life Sherlock Holmes.

The Art of Flawed Forensics

Critics say that Spilsbury was wrong as often as he was right. Although he became a celebrity and was knighted, in retrospect, many of his conclusions seem questionable. According to the *London Times*, "He sent more than one innocent to the gallows. His theories increasingly took precedence over facts. Most notorious was the 1923 case of Norman Thorne, sentenced to death for killing his girlfriend. She had almost certainly committed suicide, and the evidence was thin, but Spilsbury's testimony was unwavering."

The Quotable P.I. _____

Mike Hammer: *Everything I touch dies.* —ARMAND ASSANTE AS P.I. MIKE HAMMER IN *I, THE JURY* (1982)

No Notes for Suicide

In December 1947, Spilsbury gassed himself to death. The scientist, who had studied, investigated, and catalogued so many thousands of deaths, left no note to explain his own.

Pride Goeth Before the Fall. Or, How to Fake a Suicide

The Suicide Rules: what you use if you think you're smart enough to murder someone and make it look like a suicide.

The Suicide Rule #1: The Suicide Note. The note—you've always gotta leave the note. If you can get the victim to write the note first, that's half the battle (you can figure out what the other half is). Typed notes don't really cut it— and you could leave fingerprints on the keys. No fingerprints on the keys is even worse! Very few people, even those planning their own demise, wear gloves to type something.

The Suicide Rule #2: The Victim's Clothes. If you want to shoot him/her in the chest or stomach, make sure you remove and/or open the shirt/blouse first. Suicides tend to not shoot through clothing. Could be fear of infection but, considering the task they're undertaking, it seems a touch overkill.

The Suicide Rule #3: The Handgun. If it's a handgun, make sure it's resting close enough to the body to have been dropped there by the suicide.

The Suicide Rule #4: Powder Burns. You have to fire close enough to leave powder burns on the victim.

The Suicide Rule #5: Gunshot Residue. The victim's hands have to have gun-shot residue.

The Suicide Rule #6: Know Your Victim. Right-handed or left-handed? And did you make sure, if it's a head shot, that it's on the correct side for the dominant-handedness of the victim (right side for right-handed)?

The Suicide Rule #7: The Rifle. If you use a rifle, then make sure it's definitely close enough to the body to have been used by the victim.

The Suicide Rule #8: Slicing. If you decide that guns are too much trouble, you could use a knife instead. Did you leave the first tentative cuts that are typical of wrist cutting?

The Suicide Rule #9: Drowning. If you want to fake a drowning suicide in the bathtub, make sure the person is fully clothed. Naked drowning suicides are dead giveaways (sorry) that something's wrong—besides the obvious, that is.

The Suicide Rule #10: Hanging. A hanging suicide can't be a strangling faked to look like a hanging. The ligature marks are different from a strangling.

The Suicide Rule #11: How Smart Are You Really? All things considered, maybe you're better off just getting a divorce.

When All Else Fails, Make It Murder

If You Can't Fake a Suicide Rule #1: The Bathtub Drowning. The accidental drowning from a fall in the bathtub's an old standby, but be careful what you use to hit the victim in the head first. A cranium dent from a ball-peen hammer, for instance, looks nothing like something you'd get from slipping in the tub.

If You Can't Fake a Suicide Rule #2: The Burglar Routine. A murder by someone breaking a window to burgle a house has to leave the broken glass on the inside.

If You Can't Fake a Suicide Rule #3: Footprints. You've also got all that footprint outside business. There really should be footprints, but they'd better not be yours.

First Lines

  "The first time I met Karen Nichols, she struck me as the kind of woman who ironed her socks." —*PRAYERS FOR RAIN* (1999) BY DENNIS LEHANE

The Original Gil Grissom: *Quincy M.E.*

Given television's current fascination with everything forensics, from the *CSI* shows to *NCIS* to *Bones*, it might be worthwhile to look at an old-school show. While many detective series had depicted rudimentary physical evidence analysis such as fingerprints and bullet comparisons, *Quincy M.E.* (1976–1983) was the first to regularly present the in-depth forensic investigations that would become the hallmark of current detective shows.

Medical Examiner to the Stars

Q: What real-life Los Angeles County medical examiner was the inspiration for Dr. Quincy on *Quincy M.E.*?

A: Dr. Thomas Noguchi became famous for his often controversial conclusions. He performed autopsies on many stars—including Marilyn Monroe, Natalie Wood, and John Belushi. He also raised doubts about the official account of Robert Kennedy's assassination by showing that Sirhan Sirhan could not have fired the fatal shot. Noguchi also acted as a technical advisor on *Quincy M.E.*

> "Gentlemen, you are about to enter the most important and fascinating sphere of police work: the world of forensic medicine." —JACK KLUGMAN AS QUINCY IN *QUINCY, M.E.*

Name That Medical Examiner

Q: Do you know Quincy's first name?

A: Quincy's first name was never mentioned, though in one episode his business card was shown with the name "Doctor R. Quincy."

Back from the Dead

Quincy's romantic interest became Doctor Emily Hanover, played by Anita Gillette. They later married. In an earlier flashback episode, however, Quincy's first wife, later deceased, was played by none other than actress Anita Gillette.

Murder by the Week

"It's murder, Sam! Muurderrrr!!!!" Dr. Quincy would say.

And it was, every week. For eight years.

✎ *First Lines*

"This volume, which is the first history published of the celebrated criminal cases in America, includes the most important cases during the past eighty years." —*CELEBRATED CRIMINAL CASES OF AMERICA* (1920) BY THOMAS S. DUKE, CAPTAIN OF POLICE, SAN FRANCISCO

For the *CSI* Fans

See if you're as smart as these characters:

1. Mac Taylor
2. Tim "Speed" Speedle
3. Gil Grissom
4. Horatio Caine
5. Ryan Wolfe
6. Catherine Willows
7. Sheldon Hawkes
8. Calleigh Duquesne
9. Raymond Langston
10. Jo Danville

a. Upon arrival at the crime lab stumbles upon a dead body

b. Nicknamed "The Bug Man"; likes cockroach racing

c. Stabbed by Dick and Jane killer in last episode of a season

d. Holds a degree in physics from Tulane; alcoholic father often in rehab

e. Night shift commander; unable to find evidence of spouse's killer

f. Fired when didn't disclose a direct link to a murder suspect—rehired later

g. Lost spouse in 9/11 attacks

h. Discovered to be the parent of a sixteen-year-old illegitimate son

i. Killed in a gunfight when poor maintenance resulted in weapon malfunction

j. Child prodigy; graduated college at eighteen; board-certified surgeon by twenty-four; years of experience in emergency room

ANSWER: 1-g; 2-i; 3-b; 4-h; 5-f; 6-e; 7-j; 8-d; 9-c; 10-a

Extra Credit

Q: How many *CSI* shows have theme songs by The Who?

A: Three. *CSI* ("Who are You?"), *CSI: Miami* ("Won't Get Fooled Again"), and *CSI: New York* ("Baba O'Riley")

Stranger Than Fiction

Q: What real-life crime inspired the thinly veiled novel *Compulsion*, and the movie version that earned Best Actor awards for the three leads at the Cannes Film Festival?

A: The 1924 arrest of wealthy teenagers Nathan Leopold and Richard Loeb for the "thrill killing" of fourteen-year-old Bobby Franks. Meyer Levin changed little but the names of the real people in his 1956 novel. The 1959 movie version resulted in a triple-tie at Cannes for Orson Welles ("Jonathan Wilk"/Clarence Darrow), Dean Stockwell ("Steiner"/Leopold), and Bradford Dillman ("Straus"/Loeb). Leopold and Loeb pled guilty to kidnapping and murder, but Darrow saved them from the death penalty. Loeb was killed in a prison fight in 1936. Leopold was paroled in 1958 and lived in Puerto Rico till his death in 1971.

> *"My motive, so far as I can be said to have had one, was to please Dick. . . . He could charm anybody he had a mind to. Lots of people who thought the world of him would be surprised to know his real thoughts about them. He looked down on nearly everybody."* —NATHAN LEOPOLD, *LIFE PLUS NINETY-NINE YEARS* (1958)

Too Proud to Be a Pig, Man

Q: Which actor known as the King of Cool nearly turned down the role of a lifetime out of pride?

A: The so-called King of Cool, Steve McQueen, almost let pride get in the way of his starring in *Bullitt* (1968). It's true. McQueen almost let the blockbuster slip through his hands. He believed playing a cop might cramp his style—don't let the short-cropped hair fool you, he was a hippie at heart! The movie's central character is New York police detective Frank Bullitt, assigned to protect an underworld government witness who's scheduled to testify before an upcoming senate hearing.

"No way am I playing a cop. Those kids call 'em pigs, man. What are you trying to do to me? Why, those kids would turn on me so fast it would make your head spin!" —STEVE MCQUEEN, WHEN OFFERED THE ROLE OF LIEUTENANT BULLITT, AS WITNESSED BY HIS WIFE, NEILE, AND GOOD FRIEND, HAIRDRESSER JAY SEBRING (WHO WAS LATER MURDERED, ALONG WITH ACTRESS SHARON TATE, BY THE MANSON FAMILY)

A San Francisco Kind of Cool

After having a change of heart about the men in blue, McQueen accepted the role of Lieutenant Bullitt and delivered what many consider his best performance. Directed by the legendary Peter Yates, the movie version is set in San Francisco and would become one of McQueen's most financially successful movies, grossing a reported $80 million its first year alone (an unheard of sum in 1968). With a little help from the narrow, roller-coaster streets of San Francisco, *Bullitt* has achieved cult status not only for capturing the most suspenseful, gut-wrenching big-screen car chases of all time, but for solidifying forever McQueen's title as the King of Cool.

The Novel Was Cooler

Q: Which novel by Robert Pike was adapted into the hit *Bullitt*?

A: The excellent novel *Mute Witness* (1963) served as the basis for the Steve McQueen vehicle that has been voted the coolest movie of all time.

DEADLY DIALOGUE

Walter Chalmers: *Frank, we must all compromise.*
Bullitt: *Bullshit.*

—STEVE MCQUEEN AS LIEUTENANT FRANK BULLITT AND ROBERT VAUGHN AS WALTER CHALMERS IN *BULLITT* (1968)

COP TALK: MACHISMO SPEAKS!

John Doe: *Realize, detective, the only reason that I'm here right now is that I wanted to be.*
David Mills: *No, no, we would have got you eventually.*
John Doe: *Oh really? So, what were you doing? Biding your time? Toying with me? Allowing five innocent people to die until you felt like springing your trap? Tell me, what was the indisputable evidence you were going to use on me right before I walked up to you and put my hands in the air?*

—BRAD PITT AS DETECTIVE DAVID MILLS AND KEVIN SPACEY AS JOHN DOE IN *SE7EN* (1995)

COP TALK: MACHISMO SPEAKS!

Ben Shockley: *Now if I have suspicion a felony's been committed, I can just walk right in here anytime I feel like it, 'cause I got this badge, I got this gun, and I got the love of Jesus right here in my pretty green eyes.*

—CLINT EASTWOOD AS BEN SHOCKLEY IN *THE GAUNTLET* (1977)

A Pride of Literary Lions

Match the author called the best by the Mystery Writers of America to the police procedural written by the same:

1. *Dance Hall of the Dead* (1973)
2. *The Laughing Policeman* (1968)
3. *Gorky Park* (1981)
4. *A Thief of Time* (1988)
5. *The First Deadly Sin* (1973)
6. *Last Seen Wearing . . .* (1952)
7. *The Steam Pig* (1971)
8. *The Choirboys* (1975)
9. *Shroud for a Nightingale* (1971)
10. *Ice* (1983)
11. *In the Heat of the Night* (1965)

a. Hillary Waugh
b. Ed McBain
c. Tony Hillerman
d. Joseph Wambaugh
e. Tony Hillerman
f. Maj Sjöwall & Per Wahlöö
g. James McClure
h. Martin Cruz Smith
i. Lawrence Sanders
j. P. D. James
k. John Ball

ANSWERS: 1-e; 2-f; 3-h; 4-c; 5-i; 6-a; 7-g; 8-d; 9-j; 10-b; 11-k

Try Saying It Ten Times Fast

Q: What author, regarded as the father of Japanese detective fiction, styled his pseudonym to sound like "Edgar Allan Poe" when said quickly?

A: Edogawa Rampo was actually born Hirai Tarō. He founded the Detective Author's Club (now the Japan Detective Writer's Association) and counted Poe as an inspiration for his work—along with Sir Arthur Conan Doyle and G. K. Chesterton.

The Statement Is False

Edogawa Rampo's debut story "The Two-Sen Copper Coin" (1923) is the first piece of modern Japanese mystery fiction.

✑ First Lines

"Fukia might have gone a long way in the world if he had only put his considerable intelligence to use." —"THE PSYCHOLOGICAL TEST" (1925) BY EDOGAWA RAMPO

Get Your Stories Straight

In fact, Japanese authors such as Ruikō Kuroiwa, Kidō Okamoto, Jun'ichirō Tanizaki, Haruo Satō, and Kaita Murayama had used similar elements in their own stories. What is true? Rampo's first story pays homage to that logical deduction in a story founded in Buddhist code.

The Sensational Truth

Edogawa Rampo relied on a combination of elements known as "ero guro nansensu" ("eroticism, grotesquerie, and the nonsensical") to capture his audience's interest.

COP TALK: MACHISMO SPEAKS!

Marge Gunderson: *Say, Lou, didya hear the one about the guy who couldn't afford personalized plates, so he went and changed his name to J3L2404?* —FRANCES MCDORMAND AS POLICE CHIEF MARGE GUNDERSON IN *FARGO* (1996)

Drive, He Said

Private investigators pride themselves on their rides. To wit:

- Jim Rockford (*The Rockford Files*)
  Seasons 1–6: Pontiac Firebird Esprit
- Thomas Magnum (*Magnum, P.I.*)
  Season 1: 1978 Ferrari 308GTS

Seasons 2–3: 1980 Ferrari 308GTSi

Seasons 4–6: 1984 Ferrari 308GTSi

Seasons 7–8: 1984 Ferrari 308GTSi QV

- Joe Mannix (*Mannix*)

  Season 1: 1967 Oldsmobile Toronado roadster (1966 Mercury Comet Caliente convertible, 1967 Mercury Comet Cyclone convertible, 1967 Ford Galaxie 500 four-door hardtop, and a 1967 Ford Fairlane 500 four-door sedan all made limited appearances)

  Season 2: 1968 Dodge Dart GTS 340 convertible

  Season 3: 1969 Dodge Dart GTS 340 convertible

  Season 4: 1970 Plymouth Cuda 340 convertible

  Season 5: 1971 Plymouth Cuda 340 convertible

  Season 6: 1973 Plymouth Cuda 340 convertible

  Season 7: 1974 Dodge Challenger 360 Coupe

  Season 8: Chevrolet Camaro LT
- Frank Cannon (*Cannon*)

  Seasons 1–5: Lincoln Continental Mark IV

When Do Lone Wolves Join a Pack?

When the pack consists of other lone wolves. Two of the many organizations private investigators can join in order to network, to learn, and to bare their teeth:

- United States Association of Professional Investigators (*http://www.usapi.org*)
- Council of International Investigators (*http://www.cii2.org*)

Just Call Me Angel

Think about this the next time a nurse injects something into your IV: The Angel of Death or Angel of Mercy killer is a lethal caretaker who preys on vulnerable, dependent patients in a hospital, nursing home, or other health-care setting. Usually female, but sometimes male, the Angel of Death is difficult to detect until her number of victims grows too large to ignore.

- Average number of victims: eight known, likely at least double that and possibly into the hundreds
- Average age at first kill: twenty-six
- Active "killing" phase: two years average, but sometimes decades
- Victims of choice: elderly, infirm, children
- Method of choice: lethal injection, suffocation
- Motives: power, ego, attention

Bumbling "Hero"

Unlike most so-called Angels of Death, Richard Angelo didn't want to kill the patients he injected with paralyzing drugs. He wanted to bring them back from near-death and be hailed as a hero! Instead, of the thirty-seven patients who went "Code Blue" during his graveyard shifts at Long Island's Good Samaritan Hospital, only twelve survived.

Angelo's wings were clipped in October 1987, when patient Gerolamo Kucich caught him in the act. A urine specimen confirmed the presence of two drugs later found in Angelo's home. The bodies of other patients who'd died while under his "care" were exhumed, and ten tested positive for the drugs. Angelo is serving sixty-six years to life and probably does not get to work in the prison infirmary.

> *"I wanted to create a situation where I would cause the patient to have some respiratory distress or some problem, and through my intervention or suggested intervention or whatever, come out looking like I knew what I was doing."* —RICHARD ANGELO, TAPED CONFESSION

The Pride of the Irish

Q: Which Irish-Catholic American was celebrated in the House of Lords for such works as *The Friends of Eddie Coyle* (1972)?

A: George V. Higgins, the author of over two dozen books including Elmore Leonard's favorite crime novel, *The Friends of Eddie Coyle*, was also a noted criminal trial lawyer of national stature with the U.S. Attorney's Office and eventually his own law firm. Nevertheless, his true love was writing. In 1972 he published *The Friends of Eddie Coyle* (his first novel), which would be made into a movie starring Robert Mitchum and Peter Boyle. *Coyle* would go on to become a finalist for a National Book Award and in 1985 the British Booksellers Association voted it one of the twenty best American novels since World War II.

"You can always count on a murderer for a fancy prose style."
—VLADIMIR NABOKOV

The King of Dialogue

George V. Higgins was a powerhouse in the field of legal crime literature—and was lauded most notably for his authentic knowledge of underworld and street dialogue. Which explains why Elmore Leonard was such a fan—as he, too, was a master of what Higgins called the "nuances of ordinary speech."

Unfortunately, however, the same streetwise language that made Higgins so popular and acclaimed led his longtime mentor Mr. Kelly to express his displeasure. Kelly, a dapper, proud, old-fashioned Irish-Catholic gentleman, engaged Higgins in friendly debates over everything from sports to politics to history from the time he was a boy. Higgins very much admired his old debating partner and when *Coyle* was released he rushed down to Green

Harbor, gleaming with pride and intent on winning the old gent's approval. He presented Mr. Kelly with a copy, but when his old friend inspected the book he was scandalized to see the Lord's name taken in vain on the second page of the novel. He shook his head at Higgins, "George, I can't read this blasphemy!"

Blasphemy aside, they remained good friends.

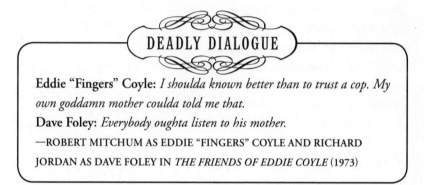

DEADLY DIALOGUE

Eddie "Fingers" Coyle: *I shoulda known better than to trust a cop. My own goddamn mother coulda told me that.*
Dave Foley: *Everybody oughta listen to his mother.*
—ROBERT MITCHUM AS EDDIE "FINGERS" COYLE AND RICHARD JORDAN AS DAVE FOLEY IN *THE FRIENDS OF EDDIE COYLE* (1973)

The World's Greatest Detective—If I Say So Myself

Agatha Christie's Belgian creation Hercule Poirot is nothing if not proud. In *The Mystery of the Spanish Chest*, murder suspect Colonel Curtiss commits the ultimate *faux pas* when he calls Poirot "a detective."

"I am *the* detective, Mr. Curtiss," Poirot says, by way of correction.

The Quotable P.I. _____

Simo: *Louis Simo. S-I-M-O.* —ADRIEN BRODY AS P.I. LOUIS SIMO IN *HOLLYWOODLAND* (2006)

Agatha by the Numbers

- According to the *Guinness Book of World Records*, there are an estimated two billion Agatha Christie books in print. (That's more than seven times J. K. Rowling's record.)
- Agatha Christie wrote:
  - Eighty novels and short story collections (including six romance novels as Mary Westmacott)
  - Nineteen plays
  - Two books of poetry
  - Two autobiographical works
  - One children's book
- Agatha Christie was the first crime writer to achieve "A Penguin Million" when the publisher printed 100,000 copies of ten of her titles on the same day in 1948.

Real Lady Killers

If Agatha Christie only killed one character in every book and play she wrote, she'd have a higher body count than Delfina and María de Jesús Gonzáles—the Mexican serial killer sisters who murdered eighty women and eleven men.

"She will appear to be going about her business in an efficient and caring manner, while in reality, she is determining who is to live and who is to die." —MURDER MOST RARE: THE FEMALE SERIAL KILLER (1998) BY MICHAEL D. KELLEHER AND C. L. KELLEHER

A Hit Too Far

Arthur Flegenheimer, AKA Dutch Schultz, was not known as a subtle, behind-the-scenes leader in the New York mob of the early 1930s. When he suspected one of his henchmen of disloyalty, he personally fitted the guy with cement overshoes and tossed him—alive—into the Hudson River. So when newly appointed special prosecutor Thomas E. Dewey set his sights on Schultz, old Dutch predictably overreacted: He announced he was going to have Dewey killed.

The wiser heads of the Commission, including Lucky Luciano and Meyer Lansky, nixed the hit. Any move on Dewey, a former federal prosecutor, would bring too much heat and might even open the door for the FBI. Dutch knew the rules: no hits on politicians and no hits without the unanimous approval of the Commission.

Dutch figured the rules didn't apply to him. Wrong. On October 23, 1935, Dutch Schultz and three associates were gunned down in Newark's Palace Chophouse and Tavern by Charlie Workman of Murder, Inc., a nickname for the mob's internal death squad.

COP TALK: MACHISMO SPEAKS!

Captain George Ellerby: *This unit is new, and you are the newest members of it. You have been selected from the basis of intelligence and aptitude. This is an elite unit. Our job is to smash, or marginally disrupt, organized crime in the city by enhanced cooperation of the FBI, represented here today by Frank Lazio. And we will do it. By organized crime in the city, you know who we mean—that's Jackie Costigan, that's an old picture. Jackie met his demise. Last known photograph. Costello uses three key guys: that's Fitzy—off-the-boat psycho who lives with his mother, who's straight out of* Going My Way. *Delahunt—muscle. French—the number one. But of course the rock star—you know who. We've done a briefing. Books, so read up. I want any and all ideas so I can pass them off as my own. Work hard, you'll rise fast. You're in the best possible position in the department. Let's go to work.*

—ALEC BALDWIN AS CAPTAIN ELLERBY IN *THE DEPARTED* (2006)

> *"Disciplining yourself to do what you know is right and important, although difficult, is the high road to pride, self-esteem, and personal satisfaction."* —MARGARET THATCHER

DEADLY DIALOGUE

Harry Lime: *In Italy, for thirty years, under the Borgias, they had warfare, terror, murder, and bloodshed. But they produced Michelangelo, Leonardo da Vinci, and the Renaissance. In Switzerland, they had brotherly love, and they had five hundred years of democracy and peace, and what did that produce? The cuckoo clock.* —ORSON WELLES AS HARRY LIME IN *THE THIRD MAN* (1949)

The Murder Exhibit

Q: What serial killer carried out his crimes against the backdrop of the 1893 Chicago World's Fair, using his World's Fair Hotel to attract victims?

A: Herman Mudgett, AKA Dr. H. H. Holmes, prided himself on being so much cleverer than his victims or the investigators who pursued him at various times for crimes ranging from fraud to child kidnapping and murder. He was so efficient at disposing of bodies that no accurate number of victims was ever determined. He was convicted of nine, confessed to more than twenty, and may have killed well over one hundred.

From Infamous to Famous

Mudgett's crimes, against the backdrop of the Chicago World's Fair, are detailed by Erik Larsen in *The Devil in the White City* (2003), winner of the 2004 Edgar Award for Best Fact Crime book.

⊗ *First Lines*

"The day was April 14, 1912, a sinister day in maritime history, but of course the man in suite 63–65, shelter deck C, did not yet know it."
—*THE DEVIL IN THE WHITE CITY* (2003) BY ERIK LARSEN

"Remorse for what? You people have done everything in the world to me. Doesn't that give me equal right?" —CHARLES MANSON

Name That Tune—Or Else

Several weeks after the 1934 deaths of Bonnie Parker and Clyde Barrow, a poem about the notorious gangster couple hit the popular press. "The Trail's End" was set to music several times as a Texas folk song, a French-language duet, and a pop single. The fatalistic lyrics, written before the deadly ambush by lawmen, predicted a bad end for the duo. According to the official coroner's report, Clyde was shot seventeen times and Bonnie twenty-six times. The poem had been given to Mrs. Parker two weeks earlier by the author—her daughter, Bonnie.

End of the Trail for Bonnie and Clyde

"Now Bonnie and Clyde are the Barrow gang,
I'm sure you all have read
How they rob and steal and how those who squeal
Are usually found dying or dead. . . .
"Some day they will go down together,
and they will bury them side by side.
For a few it means grief, for the law it's relief,
But it's death to Bonnie and Clyde."
—"THE TRAIL'S END" BY BONNIE PARKER (1934)

Flip Sides of the Same Coin?

Q: Al Pacino and Robert De Niro have only starred in three movies together. What are the movies and on what side of the law did they appear?

A: *The Godfather: Part II* (1974) where Pacino and De Niro both play gangsters; *Heat* (1995) in which Pacino plays a cop and De Niro plays a gangster; and *Righteous Kill* (2008) in which Pacino and De Niro both play cops

---

"Speak the truth and shame the devil." —ITALIAN SAYING

Top Legal Guns

Q: What are the three greatest legal movies of all time, according to the *American Bar Association Journal?*

A: *To Kill a Mockingbird* (1962), *12 Angry Men* (1957), and the 1992 comedy *My Cousin Vinny*

Italian Pride and Family Honor

When two young men from New York, Billy Gambini (Ralph Macchio) and Stan Rothenstein (Mitchell Whitfield), travel through deep Alabama, they get accused of a murder they didn't commit. Billy knows just what to do. Call his cousin, Vinny Gambini (Joe Pesci). Vinny is a tough but lovable Italian from the streets of Brooklyn who just passed the bar exam after his sixth attempt. He has no trial experience, but he has at least three things going for him:

1. Family is family and Billy knows cousin Vinny won't let him down.
2. Vinny's sexy, loyal, and extremely intelligent fiancée Mona Lisa (Marisa Tomei).
3. Vinny's intense Italian pride.

Dressed to Defend

My Cousin Vinny's trial scenes are legendary. This is in large part because of the hilarious exchanges between by-the-book judge Chamberlain Haller (Fred Gwynne) and Vinny. Much of the animosity between the two comes from Vinny's casual street attire worn in Haller's courtroom and the fact that Vinny has no understanding of Alabama criminal procedure.

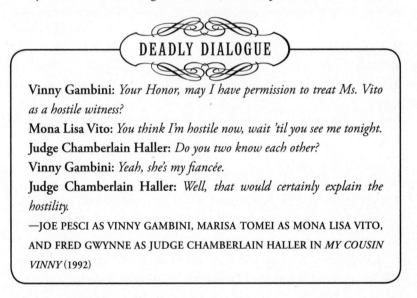

DEADLY DIALOGUE

Vinny Gambini: *Your Honor, may I have permission to treat Ms. Vito as a hostile witness?*

Mona Lisa Vito: *You think I'm hostile now, wait 'til you see me tonight.*

Judge Chamberlain Haller: *Do you two know each other?*

Vinny Gambini: *Yeah, she's my fiancée.*

Judge Chamberlain Haller: *Well, that would certainly explain the hostility.*

—JOE PESCI AS VINNY GAMBINI, MARISA TOMEI AS MONA LISA VITO, AND FRED GWYNNE AS JUDGE CHAMBERLAIN HALLER IN *MY COUSIN VINNY* (1992)

Nagging Her Way to an Oscar

Tomei's role as the ever-loyal, yet ever-nagging fiancée Mona Lisa (also a proud Italian) snagged her an Academy Award for Best Supporting Actress.

Sin, Smile, and Say You're Happy

Where's all the humor in the legal thriller? Look no further than comedic genius Henry Cecil. In addition to having some of the cleverest humor—or is it "humour"—in all of crime fiction, let alone in the literary legal field, Henry Cecil was actually a judge as well. His works often feature bumbling, silly characters and likable rogues who let petty jealousy, pride, envy, failed attempts at greed, quasi-lust, and, on occasion, murder interfere with their daily, humdrum lives.

A Funny Body of Work

His works not only create platforms for man and his folly, but are actually quite sound in law, present ingenious legal twists and, because they are based on his experiences as a circuit court judge, are quite realistic with remarkable legal twists:

- *No Bail for the Judge* (1952)
- *According to the Evidence* (1954)
- *Brothers in Law* (1955)
- *Sober as a Judge* (1958)
- *Settled Out of Court* (1959)
- *Alibi for a Judge* (1960)
- *Unlawful Occasions* (1962)
- *The Asking Price* (1966)
- *Tell You What I'll Do* (1969)
- *Juror in Waiting* (1970)

Ready for Your Close Up, Mr. Cecil DeMille?

Q: Which of Cecil's works made it to the screen?

A: His novel *Brothers in Law* was made into a film and *Alibi for the Judge* was adapted by Felicity Douglas at the Savoy Theatre in London. Even the Master of Suspense himself, Alfred Hitchcock, got his greedy little hands on Cecil's works, airing his short story "I Saw the Whole Thing" (1962) on *The Alfred Hitchcock Hour*.

> *"If I wanted to be pompous, which I often do, I would say (truthfully) that every writer I'd ever read has influenced me—and then I'd give you a list, starting with Plato."* —ELIZABETH PETERS

Move Over, Ian Fleming

International number-one bestselling author Jeffery Deaver continues to be on top of his game. Deaver, a former journalist, folksinger, and lawyer has international ties, much like his new character—the suave, dashing, heart-breaking James Bond. That's right, the Foreign Office assigned Deaver, Jeffery Deaver, the task of writing the latest James Bond novel *Carte Blanche* (2011). And "M" couldn't have chosen a better author.

Like Bond, Deaver gets around. His books appear in 150 countries and have been translated into twenty-five languages—a claim even Bond can't make. His novel *The Bone Collector* (1997) featuring ex-head of the NYPD Forensics, quadriplegic Lincoln Rhyme, went Hollywood starring Denzel Washington and Angelina Jolie. In addition to breakneck suspense, the Rhyme novels combine the best of the modern thriller with cerebral Sherlock Holmes–type detecting.

> *"I have always wanted to be liked and respected."* —O. J. SIMPSON

EPILOGUE

Dos and Don'ts of Burying the Victim

Okay, you've finally done it. After years of wanting to, you've finally killed that person that needed killing the way flowers need water. After years of wanting to, you've finally gotten rid of that person you hate. Well, not quite. You've killed the person, but stuck the body in the trunk of your car and are driving around with no idea how to get rid of it. But you're smart, you've always been smarter than anyone else.

- DO wait until dark. If it's already nighttime, you're golden.
- DON'T dump it in a river. It would float.
- DON'T underestimate its weight. As you've likely discovered while getting the stiff into your trunk, the damned thing is heavy. Dead weight, as it were.
- DON'T throw it off a bridge. The off-the-bridge thing is tricky. Cars approach bridges. From both directions.
- DO use a boat to take it out to deep water. Deep as in ocean (think *Dexter*).
- DO bury it if it's too heavy to haul out to sea.
- DON'T bury it someplace you know too well. Good example of a bad place to bury a body: a jogging area you've used. If you're a suspect, that's the first place they'd look.
- DO consider the terrain. Think wild and hilly. It's harder to search and less attractive to casual hikers.
- DON'T head downhill. Easier to move the body, but they look downhill first.
- DO take the body uphill. If you can figure out how to get the body up there.
- DON'T bury the body too shallow. Cadaver dogs can sniff it out.

- DON'T bury the body too deep. A freshly dug grave tends to leave an elevation in the ground, which after a while becomes a depression. Dig one really deep, it might be hard for the dogs to smell it out, but after a while it leaves an even deeper depression because of soil settling, body decay, and collapse of the skeleton. Also, the burial site can change. Less vegetation, or maybe more because of the turned-over dirt and the body decaying.
- DO think about this—preferably before everything goes down. The slightest mistake could be a real killer.

INDEX